ME
MYSELF
& LIES

a thought-closet makeover

JENNIFER ROTHSCHILD

LifeWay Press®
Nashville, Tennessee

Published by LifeWay Press®
©2008 · Jennifer Rothschild
Reprinted September 2018

ISBN: 978-1-4158-6644-3
Item number 005179845

Dewey Decimal Number: 155.2
Subject Areas: SELF-TALK \ SELF-PERCEPTION \
COMMUNICATION--PSYCHOLOGICAL ASPECTS

Scripture quotations, unless noted otherwise, are taken from the New American Standard Bible®, Copyright © 1960, 1962, 1963, 1968, 172, 1973, 1975, 1977, 1995 by The Lockman Foundation. Used by permission *(www. lockman.org)*. Scripture quotations marked HCSB are taken from the Holman Christian Standard Bible, copyright © 1999, 2001, 2002 by Holman Bible Publishers. Used by permission. Scripture quotations marked NKJV are from the New King James Version. Copyright Thomas Nelson, Inc., Publishers. Scripture quotations marked HCSB are taken from the Holman Christian Standard Bible, copyright © 1999, 2001, 2002 by Holman Bible Publishers. Used by permission. Scripture quotations marked NIV are from the Holy Bible, New International Version, copyright © 1973, 1978, 1984 by International Bible Society.

To order additional copies of this resource: Write LifeWay Church Resources Customer Service; One LifeWay Plaza; Nashville, TN 37234-0113; Fax order to 615.251.5933; call toll free 800.458.2772; email *orderentry@lifeway.com;* order online *www.lifeway.com;* or visit the LifeWay Christian store serving you.

Printed in the United States of America.

Adult Ministry Publishing
LifeWay Church Resources
One LifeWay Plaza
Nashville, TN 37234-0152

CONTENTS

ABOUT THE AUTHOR

The verse, "Let the words of my mouth, and the meditation of my heart, be acceptable in thy sight, O LORD, my strength, and my redeemer" (Ps. 19:14, KJV), has much to say to each of us. For Jennifer Rothschild, the words are much more than a beloved Scripture; they are a reflection of how she organizes her thought closet.

At the age of 15 Jennifer was diagnosed with a rare, degenerative eye disease that would eventually steal her sight. It was more than a turning point for the Miami, Florida, native. Her dreams of becoming a commercial artist and cartoonist faded. Words and music have replaced her canvas and palette.

Through her spiritual depth and down-to-earth style, Jennifer weaves music, illustrations, and biblical truth to help people find contentment, walk with endurance, and celebrate the ordinary. Through her storytelling and wit, they look beyond circumstances and experience God's grace in adversity.

This Bible study is based on Jennifer's trade book by the same name. She also co-founded and publishes *WomensMinistry.NET,* a popular online magazine. She and her husband, Philip, live in Springfield, Missouri, with their sons, Clayton and Connor. Jennifer enjoys nature walks, theme parks, and riding a bicycle built for two.

In addition to her writing and speaking ministry, Jennifer is an accomplished songwriter and recording artist with four albums to her credit—*Out of the Darkness, Come to the Morning, Not by Sight,* and *Live in Concert.*

Get a free copy of Jennifer's song "Let the Words" on CD or by download by visiting *www.JenniferRothschild.com/words.*

INTRODUCTION

We all know at least one woman who seems to be clothed with peace and grace. She stands out in a crowd. She's a woman whose endured hardship but hasn't become hard; has had her world shaken, but remains unshakable. Every wave of difficulty that has washed over her has polished and revealed in her that something special we all want. Such women are rare, but God placed just enough around to salt the earth with them and make the rest of us thirsty.

I want to tell you. You can be that woman.

She's not superman in a skirt. She's a woman like you and me who has learned a transcendent truth and she practices it daily. She's learned to speak truth to her soul, and it's reflected in the wardrobe of her life. In the coming pages we're going to consider what I call our thought closets. By the end I pray we'll have filled ours with garments of truth that make us radiant just like the beautiful person she is.

My hope is that we'll support each other as sisters and learn together to be more like that radiant woman. We'll gain real and lasting freedom from some lies that have tormented us. We'll receive some mastery over the thoughts that once imprisoned us. We'll move a few steps down the path the apostle Paul called the "renewing of your mind."

Each week, you'll begin your group time with a video. I'll share some teaching from Scripture, and you'll get to meet some of my friends. You'll even get a peek into their thought closets. Then I'll turn the discussion over to your group while I enjoy some Scripture in my ears and coffee in my cup.

Please don't forget to save some final moments in your group time to invite me back. I'll wrap up our time together with a final word or two and even a fun invitation that you don't want to miss!

During the week, I look forward to spending daily time with you in the Scriptures. I'm so glad we're going to make this journey together. I wish I could be there in every sense, but this workbook and the videos provide the best alternative. Have a blessed journey, and I'll see you in the first session.

When we meet, we'll recognize each other because we're going to become "that woman!" Bring it on!

intro session
LISTENING GUIDE

We are capable of making it well with our souls based on what we _____ to tell ourselves.

We have the potential of saying things to _____ that we would never say to anyone else.

Your thought closet was designed to host _____ matters.

The words of your mouth include the ones you speak to your _____ _____.

The standard for our self-talk is what is _____ to God.

God is the _____ and strength for your self-talk.

Every wrong word and every lie that is spoken can be _____ by God.

CONVERSATION GUIDE
1. How would you describe your self-talk? Constructive, destructive, ineffective, powerful?
2. What do you hope to experience/achieve from this study?
3. Which of the C-L-O-S-E-T sections give you the most problems?

Video sessions are available for download at *www.lifeway.com/women*

WHAT'S IN YOUR THOUGHT CLOSET?

Let the words of my mouth,

and the meditation of my heart,

be acceptable in thy sight,

O LORD, my strength,

and my redeemer.

PSALM 19:14, KJV

Have you ever considered that what you say to yourself is important? Hi, this is Jennifer Rothschild, and I'm so glad you're joining me for this study. Often the words we speak to ourselves while lying in bed or looking into the mirror are not even close to the words God wants us to speak to our souls.

We tell ourselves lies like "You're so stupid" or "You're never going to change." That just won't do! So, let's learn how to speak truth to our souls. Here's a hint about what we will do over the next few weeks: we'll recognize what we say to ourselves, begin to refuse the lies we speak to ourselves, and replace that old destructive self-talk with powerful, life-changing soul talk that comes straight from the pages of Scripture.

It's what I call a thought closet makeover! Hmmm … don't know what a thought closet is? You will after starting this study! So, let's go!

My friend, I know God led you here. I've prayed for you and can't wait to hear how God teaches and guides you into truth—I know He will. I'd love for you to introduce yourself to me at my blog *www.selftalksoultalk.com*.

Day 1
NOT SO WELL WITH MY SOUL

"It is well with my soul." If you've done my *Walking by Faith* Bible study, you know that's my theme … it doesn't have to be well with your circumstances to be well with your soul. Since God planted that truth in my heart many years ago, it continues to blossom and grow. I speak on the theme "It is well with my soul" often, either in a small group in my church or in front of thousands. I really mean it—it *is* well with my soul.

But here's the deal. Every time I sing that beloved song, the chorus demands I boldly proclaim "it is well" no less than three times—whether I feel that way or not!

I couldn't count how many times I've sung those words after speaking, only to sit back down and feel a complete lack of wellness with my soul. You should hear some of the unkind words I've said to myself. *You should have done a better job.*

Listen to that speaker. She's so much smarter than you.

Oh, my friend, I could go on and on. My steady flow of disapproving thoughts and self-talk once formed a constant stream running through my mind. I badgered, devalued, and said cutting words to myself. Does this sound familiar to you?

Harsh words can feel like a raging river, tossing us until we feel we're drowning in our own self-condemnation. But sometimes our destructive self-talk is more like a steady drip-dripping—an unrelenting trickle of poison, creating a wash of pessimism. The words you speak to your own soul really can make it "well" or "not so well" with your soul. Why? Because words have great influence … even the ones you silently speak to yourself. That's why it matters how you use them.

> Even silently spoken words have great influence. It matters how you use them.

What do Genesis 1:3,6,9,11,14,20,24 reveal about how God uses words?

God used His words to create. He spoke things into being. Our words have influence, but only God's words have power. Our words don't create or destroy, but they do promote life as they build up or death as they tear down our emotions and disturb our spiritual growth.

I gave you a glimpse of the influence of my own words. How about you? Think about what your words are doing. Just think; don't write them down.

Proverbs 18:21 describes two distinct outcomes of our words. What are they?

What are some words that breathe life into you?

What words throw a shroud of death over you?

Use forms of these words to complete these statements:

My words can bring (life words) _____

My words can lead to (death words) _____

Don't assume only the words you speak aloud either bring life or invite death. The silent words you speak to your own soul are just as important.

Words convey thoughts. Words frame thoughts; thoughts consist of words. We can't even think without words, and you can't talk to yourself without using words! That's why we're first going to pay attention to how we use words.

Matthew 12:34 says, "The mouth speaks from the overflow of the heart" (HCSB). According to this verse, who you are and what's in your heart are revealed in the words you speak. Think again about the words you use.

Matthew 12 records words between Jesus and the Pharisees. The Pharisees spewed ugly words because their hearts were ugly; our Master voiced beautiful words because His heart was beautiful. Jesus used the Pharisee's confrontation to contrast the influence of words and their origin.

> Who you are and what's in your heart are revealed in the words you speak.

"A good man produces good things from his storeroom of good, and an evil man produces evil things from his storeroom of evil" (v. 35). The Greek word for *storeroom* is *thesauros.* The term *thesaurus,* used to describe a storeroom (collection) of words, is derived from this word. *Thesauros* also refers to the magi's chests of gold, frankincense, and myrrh (Matt. 2:11).

A *thesauros,* like a storeroom or the magi's chests, is a container. Your heart and mind are also containers. They are full of words, many of which you've said to yourself over the years. When people used words in Scripture, it reflected what was in their *thesauros.*

We use all sorts of words to express who we are. These words in our treasure chest consist of roles, nationalities, positions, personality traits, opinions, emotional conditions, physical traits, and even spiritual conditions.

Compile a thesaurus for the various biblical characters in these passages. Notice that most of the identifying contents begin with "I am."

Genesis 24:24—*I am* _____

Genesis 24:34—*I am* _____

Genesis 27:2—*I am* _____

Genesis 29:33—*I am* _____

Exodus 4:10—*I am* _____

Song of Songs 1:5—*I am* _____

We also use *I am* to identify ourselves. But consider the "why" behind the "who." Let's park here with Moses for a minute.

> **Why do you think Moses chose that "I am" (Ex. 4:10)?**

Moses identified himself by his stutter, his struggle. Ponder that for a moment.

> **What else do you know about Moses that could have identified him?**

We often choose our "I am" based on what we do and our struggles.

> **Now, peek into the psalmist's *thesauros* and fill in the "I am's" to see if he did the same.**
>
> **Psalm 86:2—***I am* _____
>
> **Psalm 139:14—***I am* _____
>
> **Did the psalmist's *thesauros* reflect what he might have felt was true or what actually was true?**

So what's in your *thesauros?* If you could think of your heart and mind as a book containing lots of words—list below some of the words that would fill the pages. Remember, most begin with the words *I am.* For example, open my *thesauros,* and here are the words that fly off the page: *I am ... wife, blind, sincere, loyal, insecure. (Yes, I am! I'll tell you more later!)*

In the blanks below, name some nouns that describe you—wife, daughter, and so forth:

I am ... _____

Now list adjectives that characterize you—fun, smart, impatient, and so forth:

I am ... _____

You just showed yourself what is in your *thesauros*. Aside from objective words like *mother* and *friend,* look at what you wrote.

Circle the categories below that best represent the types of words you use to identify yourself.

positive	truthful	condemning	impatient
prideful	destructive	neutral	harsh
scolding	realistic	kind	cheerful

If your heart has been made new through Christ's gift of salvation, your *thesauros* should be teeming with treasure. Review your list. Are you overflowing with words of truth, kindness, and hope? Or does your *thesauros* need some major editing? Don't be discouraged if you are disappointed with your list.

What does 1 Corinthians 15:10 say about your identity?

Before you go on, rest in His grace.

In the margin write a prayer of gratefulness for God's grace that makes you who you are. Ask Him for the grace to refine your *thesauros* so it looks more like a treasure chest than a junk yard!

The magi's treasure chest existed to have something to give Jesus. As we begin to speak wise words to our souls, we do so to ultimately have fitting treasure to offer our King. He deserves our finest thoughts, best words, and a *thesauros* full of truth.

The Enemy of your soul would love to stifle you with self-condemnation, lies, and ill-fitting words so your thoughts become a jumbled mess that controls you. He would love for you to keep listing the same old negative, untruthful stuff you've always listed. He would love to keep throwing junk into that potential treasure chest so there's no room for truth.

Girl, no more. We are going to start digging into our *thesauros* and discerning what is true about us. In fact, I like to think of our *thesauros* as a thought closet! We'll talk about that tomorrow. In the meantime, ponder this statement: *Who I am and what I struggle with are not the same thing.*

As you go through the rest of this day, ask God to show you if you have filled your *thesauros* based on who you truly are or if you have confused your identity with your struggles.

Ponder and pray about that, and we'll deal more with it in the coming weeks.

> Who I am and what I struggle with are not the same thing.

Day 2
YOUR THOUGHT CLOSET

I remember the morning I discovered how influential my words can be. I awoke to a deluge of unexpected and unsolicited quandaries. Before my feet hit the floor, I had scolded myself about my poor parenting job with my teenage son and questioned whether my toddler was getting enough attention.

"I'm not a good mom!" "I'm such a failure." Ugh. Does that ever happen to you? Of course it does!

Write down the "I am" statements you say when you're beating yourself up.

I am _____ .
I am _____ .
I am _____ .

If you beat yourself up with words, you know how I felt that morning. *Guilty. Hopeless. Frustrated.*

What words best describe how you feel when you beat yourself up?

I lugged myself into the kitchen, clothed in despair with gloomy clouds hovering overhead. I sank into a chair at the table, sipped hot tea, and tried to unknot my tangled emotions.

Was my brain simply an involuntary muscle, twitching and cramping, causing me to think on things that were not my choosing? Why couldn't I control the gray matter beneath my color-treated hair and between my own pierced ears?

You've probably felt that way too. Pull up a chair and join me in a sip of tea. Let's try to unknot this mess! Think about it. Is it really possible to control our thoughts?

How in control are you over your thoughts?
○ **completely**   ○ **most of the time**
○ **infrequently**   ○ **My thoughts control me.**

Are you satisfied with your answer? _____
Why or why not?

Yesterday we considered the thesaurus of words and thoughts tucked away in our hearts and minds. Our collection becomes our souls' vocabulary, so when our thoughts are out of control, it feels like our storerooms are bursting with a tangled mess of emotions. This thesaurus is much like a secret closet in your mind—a *thought closet.* (It's more fun to call it a closet, and it's easier to pronounce than *thesaurus!*) All those "I am's" we say to ourselves take up residence like old prom dresses, and we clothe ourselves every day with whatever we store there.

That morning I was wearing all the destructive "I am's" and untruths hidden in there, whether I wanted to or not. The shelves were jam-packed with bins full of hidden thoughts, secret insecurities, lies, and reminders of former failures.

The boxes in my thought closet had labels such as: *I'm not good enough. I'm not the wife I should be. I should have done a better job.* One unsightly shelf was stacked with bins brimming with destructive deliberations, such as: *It's all about me. I can't do it; it's impossible. I'll always be this way.*

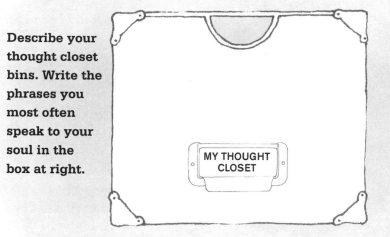

Describe your thought closet bins. Write the phrases you most often speak to your soul in the box at right.

We'll examine three closets: yours, humans' in general, and God's. You've already designed yours. Now let's check out a human thought closet when God hasn't been invited in.

On the bins below, describe what each verse says about the potential of human thought.

HUMAN THOUGHT CLOSET

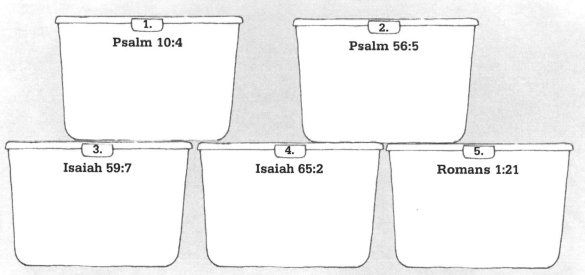

1.
Psalm 10:4

2.
Psalm 56:5

3.
Isaiah 59:7

4.
Isaiah 65:2

5.
Romans 1:21

These bins reveal how damaging human thought can be without God's control.

Place an X next to the box you relate to most and then use its Scripture to answer the following questions.

Psalm 40:5
"Many, O LORD my God, are the wonders which You have done, And Your thoughts toward us; There is none to compare with You. If I would declare and speak of them, They would be too numerous to count."

Psalm 92:5, NKJV
"O LORD, how great are Your works! Your thoughts are very deep."

Psalm 139:17, NKJV
"How precious also are Your thoughts to me, O God! How great is the sum of them!"

Isaiah 55:9
"As the heavens are higher than the earth, So are My ways higher than your ways And My thoughts than your thoughts."

Jeremiah 29:11, NKJV
"I know the thoughts that I think toward you, says the LORD, thoughts of peace and not of evil, to give you a future and a hope."

What does this verse say about the tendency of human thoughts?

Describe a time when this kind of thinking showed up in your life and how it felt.

Have you ever pulled from the human thought closet? How did your thoughts affect others?

We're capable of having a very dark thought closet without the light of Christ illuminating our minds. Now contrast the potential of human thoughts with the reality of God's thoughts.

GOD'S THOUGHT CLOSET
Fill in the boxes describing God's thoughts.

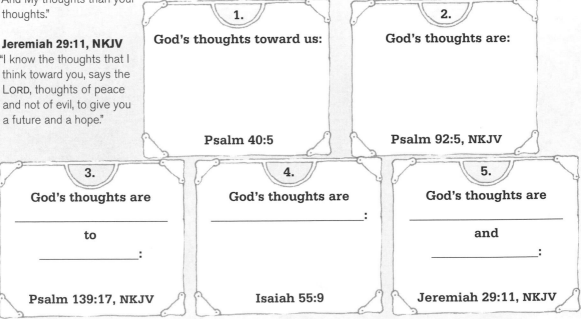

1. God's thoughts toward us:

Psalm 40:5

2. God's thoughts are:

Psalm 92:5, NKJV

3. God's thoughts are
_____
to
_____ :

Psalm 139:17, NKJV

4. God's thoughts are
_____ :

Isaiah 55:9

5. God's thoughts are
_____
and
_____ :

Jeremiah 29:11, NKJV

God's thoughts are not like our thoughts. Man's thought closet can be crammed with dark words; God's can only be full of light because He is Light.

Since you clothe your life with the contents of your thought closet, what would your life look like if you were clothed with the contents of God's thoughts?

Look back at how you filled in "My Thought Closet." Do the contents look like they draw most from...
○ **human thought**   ○ **God's thoughts?**

In what ways does your thought closet need to look more like God's?

My friend, don't be discouraged if your thought closet needs updating. Mine did, and it still requires daily maintenance! God is familiar with your thought closet. He knows what's there. He can transform your thoughts to be more like His.

Place your name in the blanks below and pray this out loud. Then speak this truth to your soul so it will be placed in your thought closet to begin the makeover.

O LORD, you have searched _____
  and you know _____.
You know when _____ sits and when _____ rises;
  you perceive _____'s thoughts from afar.
You discern _____'s going out and _____'s lying
  down; you are familiar with all _____'s ways.
Before a word is on _____'s tongue
  you know it completely, O LORD (Ps. 139:1-4, NIV).

God knows our thoughts and words, every one of them. He knows even before we do. And He can help your dilapidated thought closet experience a divine makeover!

So how does that happen? How do we fill our thought closets with words and thoughts worth wearing? Answer the following two questions to get started.

How can you establish godly thinking (Prov. 16:3)?

What does Hebrews 4:12 suggest as the true source of discerning your thoughts?

Commit
and rely.

It's possible to gain control over your thoughts. God knows your needs, and God's Spirit grants you control. The make-over starts with your awareness and commitment. It's time to update your closet's wardrobe, so commit your way to God and rely on His powerful Word. Circle the words *commit* and *rely*.

That's all I want you to do today. Don't assume it's a small task just because it's only two things! As you talk to yourself today, tell yourself to commit your way to God—one word, one thought at a time—and tell your soul to rely on God's Word more than your words. If one of your Bible study buddies calls and asks, "What's up?" you say, "I'm committing my way to God and relying on His Words, not mine!"

Day 3

THE SOUNDTRACK IN YOUR THOUGHT CLOSET

The older I get, the more I hear the words of my sweet, Southern grandmother echo through my thought closet. "Mama" taught me a lot through her words and her life. I giggle now at one of her stern admonishments. With her Southern drawl, she would say, "Honey, don't ever watch so-poppers."

As a young girl, I vowed I would not—even though I had no earthly idea what they were! I did notice each time my petite Mama preached her anti-so-popper doctrine, she was sipping a Coca-Cola® and watching *Days of Our Lives!* Not until I was a young woman did I realize what she was warning against. As thick as sweet Southern molasses, her Georgia accent had swallowed up the words *soap operas*.

That's great advice from my grandmother, but even greater wisdom comes from her often-quoted favorite psalm.

Let the words of my mouth,
and the meditation of my heart,
be acceptable in thy sight,
O Lord, my strength, and my redeemer (Ps. 19:14, KJV).

I love that prayer and the psalmist's two basic assumptions from which he prayed: humans use words and humans meditate.

We've talked about the words we use, and yesterday you thought and prayed about committing your way to God and truly relying on His Word. To put our commitment into practice, we begin today discerning the "meditations of our hearts."

Do you meditate? Mark the response that best fits you:
○ **yes**   ○ **no**   ○ **I don't know how.**
○ **I think so.**   ○ **daily**   ○ **seldom**
○ **never have; never will**   ○ **Isn't that New Age?**

Grab a dictionary or thesaurus and write some words that show up next to "meditation" or "meditate."

We all meditate, but not all of us realize it! Meditation is like our thought closets' soundtrack. We don't just hear it, we sing along.

Our meditation is made up of words, words compose thoughts, and thoughts gravitate to themes that string together, making a constant stream. It's a subconscious way of keeping our thought closets well-stocked, and it's important to tune in to the lyrics, melody, and style of our meditations.

The Hebrew word *siyach* appears several times translated as "meditate." It means "to ponder, to converse with oneself." Find the word *meditate* in the following verses.

What did the psalmist talk to himself about (Ps. 119)?

Verse 27: I will (meditate) talk to myself about
Verse 48: I will talk to myself about
Verse 78: I will talk to myself about
Verse 148: I will talk to myself about

Most of us really want to meditate, or talk to ourselves, about God's wonders and Word, but we fight the urge to meditate on

Our meditations reflect whatever we focus our minds on.

other things. Here are some of my frequent meditations: "I hope I can get my needs met." "I wonder what will happen?" "I don't know if I can get everything done!" "I am over-whelmed." and "I wish I hadn't said that stupid thing." Our meditations reflect whatever we focus our minds on.

Write on the shelf of your thought closet what you most meditate on.

Most of our meditations are swimming around in our thought closet. If you observe them, you can determine they fall into some categories—like bins in our thought closets.

My needs

My body

My plans

My insecurities

My fears

My pride

My future

My faith

My rights

My family

My wishes

My situation

My failures

Other needs

My past

The condition of our world

Circle the labeled bins at left that best characterize your most frequent meditations.

You've got bins. I've got bins. All God's children got bins! We meditate on many things, and that reveals where our thoughts are focused. That's why you circled the labeled bins.

If we are to commit our way to God so we can begin godly thinking, we must know exactly what fills our thought closets. To make our thought closets look like God's, we engage in godly meditation. First, we must focus our minds.

Colossians 3:2 tells us where to fix our minds. Read the verse and circle the words that best describe where our minds are to be focused:

Positive things—Optimism

Earthly events below

Heavenly truths above

Yesterday, we saw that God's thoughts are higher than our thoughts (Isa. 55:8-9).

How did God describe His thoughts (v. 9)?

Did you notice that Paul told us to focus our minds on things *above* and God described His thoughts as *above?*

We tend to be conversant about things beneath, while God dwells and meditates on things above. To begin to have a thought closet that looks like God's, we must have a soundtrack playing within that is written in the highest key possible! Meditation is based on things above, not on things below.

As you commit your way to God and rely on His Word, you begin to supply the content of your meditation with that which the Israelite psalmist did in Psalm 119—God's wonders and God's Word. This will focus your mind on things above.

Stop and ask God to help you focus.

Jot down in the two columns below some things you can begin to focus on:

GOD'S WONDERS   **GOD'S WORD**

In Luke 2:19, Mary showed us how to focus our minds and meditate on God's wonders and His Word. After receiving the life-changing (and world-changing!) truth she would bear the Son of God, Mary treasured and pondered all these things in her heart. The original Greek denotes that she conferred with herself and brought all her experiences and God's wonders together in her mind. Wow. That's what godly meditation looks like. Can you imagine the music in her thought closet?

Mary not only thought about the events she'd just experienced, she also made sure she remembered them. Meditation involves not only "storing" our thoughts *(kept and treasured)* like Mary did, but also "studying" them *(pondered)*.

Mary stored away and studied God's wonders and Word. How about you?

Describe one thing you stored away in your thought closet that reminds you of God's wonders or His Word:

Now before you go on, take a moment to study what you wrote. Meditate on what God did. Ponder His goodness.

As you pondered God's goodness, were you able to meditate on anything else at the same time (like your plans, your worries, your insecurities)?
○ **yes**   ○ **no**

When we meditate on God's wonders and Word, we have little room in our thought closet for anything else! We enjoy a thought closet stocked with truth. My friend, what you tuck into your thought closet will become the wardrobe of your life.

Read Psalm 119:99. What is one of the results of meditating on God's Word?

Meditating on God's wonders and His Word elevates your thoughts. It sets your mind on things above. You are not bound to earthly wisdom, but have the music of majesty and the lyric of our Lord filling your thought closet! When you find your mind wandering toward earthly things that distract you from God's wonders and Word, fix your mind on things above!

This doesn't mean helping your kids with homework, solving a daily-life dilemma, or taking a sales call is ungodly. It just means you start paying attention to where your thoughts wander during an idle moment. We will deal with this more tomorrow. Oh, your thought closet is gonna be looking good!

Day 4

SOMETHING ELSE TO THINK ABOUT

Yesterday when you tuned in to your thoughts, what did you discover? Is your thought closet full of God's Word and wonders? Did you meditate in a way that surprised you?

What did your mind's "soundtrack" consist of yesterday (or just now)?

Are you surprised at your self-talk or by the substance of what you say to yourself? I was surprised when I first tuned in to my thoughts because I used to think I didn't meditate until I realized I did it unconsciously all the time—I worried. The soundtrack in my thought closet wasn't a running "Top 20" of God's wonders and Word; it was my worries. You know, worries like: *What if I can't get a ride to my appointment? What if I fail? What if something happens to my kids?*

What do worrying and meditating have in common?

In your own words, describe worry:

Worry is fixating or meditating on *what if* rather than *what is*. Our English word *worry* comes from the Old English *wyrgan* and the Old High German *würgen*. Both mean "to strangle." When we worry, we choke out the life-giving truth that should be filling our thought closets.

   The psalmist Asaph was a celebrated musician in David's time and a leader of the temple music (1 Chron. 16:5,7). He was definitely a singer and most likely a writer of several psalms that reveal what was in his thought closet.

On what did Asaph meditate (Ps. 77:11-12)?

Pondering the goodness of God and His past provisions, like Asaph did, is a form of godly meditation. Focusing your mind

> Pondering God's goodness and past provisions is a form of godly meditation.

> Jesus reveals *what is* and therefore tells us not to worry.

YOUR THOUGHT CLOSET

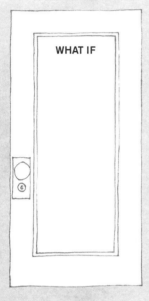

WHAT IF

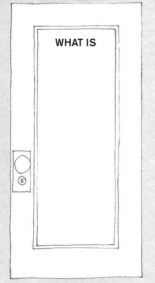

WHAT IS

on God's current provision, promises, and presence, as Mary did, is also a way to meditate. These focus our minds on truth.

Ruminating on the "what if's" is an unhealthy way of meditating that invites fear. When we do this, there's no room left in our thought closets for truth. Most worry thoughts begin with the words *what if*. Meditation on truth begins with *what is*. Jesus reveals *what is* and therefore tells us not to worry.

According to Jesus' words, what are the reasons we shouldn't worry (Matt. 6:25-32)?

What you wrote are just some of the *what is* that you should be meditating on.

On the thought closet doors at left, write your "what if" temptations to worry. Then write the corresponding "what is"—the truth from God's Word—that can fill your meditation instead.

Worry-filled meditation never leads to liberty. It turns your thought closet into a prison filled with life-choking weeds. That's why God warns against dwelling on anxious thoughts.

Turn to Philippians 4:8 to help focus your meditation. Write the categories within which we should meditate:

If it is _____, I will meditate on it.

If it is _____, I will think about it today.

If it is _____, I will dwell on it today.

If it is _____, I will fix my thoughts on it.

If it is _____, I will give it shelf space in my thought closet.

If it is ____ _____ _____, I will meditate on it today.

If it is _____, I will let it be the soundtrack in my thought closet.

If it is _____ _____ _____, I will deliberate on it today.

Compare your thought closet containing the what if's with the eight categories of meditation in Philippians 4:8. How do your anxious thoughts line up with them?
○ They fit.   ○ They don't fit.

Do the "what if's" belong in your thought closet?
○ yes   ○ no   Why or why not?

Look at the "what is" section of your closet. How do those truths line up with Philippians 4:8?
○ They fit.   ○ They don't fit.

Do they belong in your thought closet?   ○ yes   ○ no Why or why not?

God made a way to manage the meditation of your heart. From Psalm 19:14 see if you can discern:

1. The standard we should meet with our words and meditation—

2. The source from whom our words and meditation should depend—

The standard for our words and meditation is not merely what is acceptable to us; rather, it is what is acceptable to God. In our own sight, our self-talk and meditation may appear fine, but imagine God listening to you talk to yourself.

Consider God your passenger as you drive and meditate on anxious thoughts stored in your thought closet. See Him as you look in the mirror and think on old destructive thoughts. Simply put, He stands in the center of your thought closet. Imagine everything you say to yourself is spoken in His sight.

Would you still say the same things to yourself and carry on the same meditation?

What do Psalm 55:17 and 94:9 assure us God does?

> God cares about what you say to yourself because He cares about you.

My friend, God cares about your meditations. He cares about what you say to yourself because He cares about you. He is your Father, the One who made you. To focus on "what if" and never meditate on "what is" imprisons you. To dwell on untruths is to hold His truth in low regard. May it never be!

Ask God to show you if the contents and soundtracks of your thought closet are acceptable to Him. What do you believe God is showing you about this?

Scripture shows what God does for us when our meditation is worry-filled.

What does God do for us in our worries (Ps. 94:19)?

God's comfort can delight us when we are tempted to worry. The Hebrew for delight is *sha'a* and means "to look upon fondly or please oneself by looking upon something." What your soul focuses on, what you set your mind on, is what will form the bulk of your meditation. When anxious thoughts start to crowd you, shift your gaze. Expect God's consolation (comfort, relief, support, solace) to give your soul something better to focus on.

My sister, God will console and delight you when you are worried, but what does Philippians 4:6 also tell you you can do when the "what if's" begin to crowd you?

If I were sitting at your kitchen table with you right now, I would take your hand and ask, "What are you worrying about/meditating on today?" Let's tune up the soundtracks in our thought closets. Let's put them in a higher key.

Pause and form those anxious thoughts into a prayer:

**Dear Father,
Today, these "what if's" are filling my thought closet:**

I will now focus my meditation on You and Your provision:

Because You are all I wrote and so much more, I will now focus on "what is." Please make Your comfort my soul's delight. Assure me of Your promises and presence. Be big in my thought closet today. Amen.

As you close the book today, open your mind to these deliberations: Is your meditation choking you? What does God hear in your thought closet? Is it acceptable to Him? How can God's comforts delight your soul right now?

If you start to play the soundtrack of worry today in your thought closet, push the pause button and notice that the song isn't played in the key of truth. So turn your worry into a prayer. That will focus your mind on things above and invite God's comfort to delight your soul.

Day 5
WHAT DOES TRUTH SOUND LIKE?

My Bible is the size of a deck of cards, and it talks! By pressing a series of buttons, I can navigate Scripture and have "Precise Pete," my favorite digital voice, read the passage. Because it's so portable, I can truly say "Thy Word have I hid in my … purse!" Having my Bible at my fingertips makes meditation on truth easier and helps me rely on Scripture to influence my soul talk. I can carry a lot more of God's Word in my purse than I can carry in my heart, because I don't have the whole Bible memorized! And let's face it, few of us (if any) do!

If we don't have every word from all 66 books stored in our thought closets, how will we know the truths to tell ourselves, and how will we know on what to meditate? The best way, of course, is to commit as much of God's Word to memory as possible. But we don't speak to ourselves with Scripture quotes all day long. We don't supply our meditations with "thus saith the Lord" and nothing else. Let's be practical. Try to memorize Scripture. You can start with the Soul Talk Soundbites each week. But you can also become acquainted with the "sound" of truth … let's find out today what truth sounds like so you will be better equipped to recognize it.

Jesus showed us what truth sounds like as He stood in the synagogue on the Sabbath to teach.

> **How did the crowd respond to Jesus' message and describe His words (Luke 4:22)? Circle the words below that best describe …**
>
> **their response: complimentary, amazed, angry, curious, apathetic, astonished**
>
> **His words: boring, interesting, gracious, fitting, inaccurate, kind**
>
> **What was their response to Jesus in a Capernaum synagogue (v. 32)?**

My friend, our Master's words were gracious and authoritative. People were astonished when they heard His Words.

> **Think of the words you speak to your soul.**
> **Are they typically gracious?**
> ○ **yes**   ○ **no**   ○ **sometimes**   ○ **rarely**
>
> **Do they carry the authority of truth?**
> ○ **yes**   ○ **no**   ○ **sometimes**   ○ **rarely**

Truth is always authoritative and gracious. Authoritative words should never be harsh, and gracious words should never be without power.

What two qualities characterized Jesus (John 1:14,17)?

How have you experienced Jesus' gracious words in your life?

Recount a time when Jesus' truth confronted you:

Christ is grace and truth, and He is our standard. That means your soul talk is to be permeated with grace and truth. If it's not gracious, stop talking to yourself that way. Throw those thoughts out of your thought closet. If it's not truth, stop meditating on it.

> Christ is grace and truth, and He is our standard.

The standard of grace and truth is to be posted on the door of our thought closets: "Only grace and truth allowed in!" That means if you have the tendency toward name-calling, you might need a sign on the door that reads: "Do Not Enter!"

"Idiot" is the name I most often called myself when I blew it. I'll be honest. If I am really tired, stressed, or just in the Enemy's firing range, "idiot" is still the word that bangs on the door of my thought closet. Lots of us have harsh names we call ourselves. Do you? Loser. Stupid. Fat. Oh, my friend, it hurts to type those words. "Idiot" is not gracious; it is harsh. "Idiot" is also destructive, and it's not true! It is not based on the authority of Scripture. I can't afford to hang that kind of untruth in my closet, and neither can you. It's too easy to retrieve and too hard to relinquish.

When we call ourselves names, it's like getting a big, thick, black marker and writing that name on your least favorite sweater (imagine it's two sizes too small and wool!), then putting that sweater on and wearing it on the hottest day in July! And we wonder why we have bad days! Remember, you will wardrobe your life with what is in your thought closet.

What do you call yourself and how do you feel when you clothe yourself with ill-fitting words that are neither true nor gracious? Remember John 8:32 says the truth will free us. When you wardrobe yourself with one of the names hanging in your thought closet, you feel imprisoned because it isn't true or gracious! Believe me, I've been bound by badly chosen words, and I know how stifling they can be.

Sister, here's a hard truth. To call yourself an untruthful, harsh name is a sin. It's an insult to God, demeans His workmanship, and devalues His creation. On day 1 I asked you to consider the statement: "Who you are and what you struggle with are not the same thing." When you call yourself a name, it reflects what you struggle with; it is an emotional reaction. It is not a statement of who you are. Seeing the truth of what name-calling really is helps me to control my self-talk when I get frustrated with myself. I don't want to insult or hurt God.

Confess your sin of name-calling to God.

Dear Father,
Please forgive me for calling myself _____
_____.

In Your strength, I repent from telling lies to and about myself. Please give me grace to speak truth to my soul about who I am in You. I know the Enemy will tempt me in this area. Make me alert and strong in Your power. Thank You for Your forgiveness and freedom. Amen.

Hey! You finished a whole week of this study. Way to go! I know it's a daunting task to peek into your thought closet and recognize it needs some updating. But take it a word at a time, a thought at a time, a prayer at a time. Next week we will begin to relabel things. Until then, when you talk to yourself, ask: Are my words gracious and truthful?

Ponder this during the day … to be like Christ is to be full of grace and truth. If you are a name-caller, meditate on these Scriptures:

> To be like Christ is to be full of grace and truth.

"Do not let kindness and truth leave you;
Bind them around your neck,
Write them on the tablet of your heart" (Prov. 3:3).

"For my mouth will utter truth;
And wickedness is an abomination to my lips" (Prov. 8:7).

"A truthful witness gives honest testimony,
    but a false witness tells lies" (Prov. 12:17, NIV).

session one
LISTENING GUIDE

Bricks are used to make a name for _____.

_____ are man-made, but _____ are God-made.

When you and I choose to _____ ourselves,
we _____ ourselves.

We were never designed to be brick-makers; we were designed
to be _____ _____.

God desires that our lives be made up of _____
_____ that is acceptable to Him.

God labels us as " _____ _____" with the words "I AM."

God says that we are His _____,
His valued daughters.

CONVERSATION GUIDE
1. What "I am" thought has been in your Thought Closet
   the longest? Is it true?
2. Does it belong? Should you keep it?
3. What do most women make their bricks with? What do
   you use? Status, relationships, talents ...

FILLING YOUR THOUGHT CLOSET WITH TRUTH

We are destroying speculations and every lofty thing

raised up against the knowledge of God, and we are

taking every thought captive to the obedience of Christ.

2 CORINTHIANS 10: 5, NASB

Sneak a peek into Marilyn Meberg's thought closet ...

My friend Marilyn is a counselor, author, and speaker who has taught me much about the influence of our words. She knows the importance of giving ourselves truthful, gracious counsel. I asked her about how to know when we are being constructive or destructive in our self-talk and what she does when she talks to herself.

"I take myself into my office and have a chat. And when I come out, I either want my money back, or I'll say, 'You know, that was good.' That's constructive, not condemning, though. As you know, some levels of self-condemnation are damaging.

"Sometimes I need the correction. Sometimes I need the discipline. Sometimes I need to own the truth. That's instruction. That's good for me. That builds me up. But when I feel condemned, like I'm not good enough, that's not instructive. That's destructive. Instruction brings life, condemnation brings destruction."

For more of Marilyn's thoughts, visit *Selftalksoultalk.com.*

Day 1
LABEL MAKERS

Dennis confessed one of his deepest hurts. "I have three brothers," he told his friend Amy. "When my father introduced us, he said my brothers' names; and then he always said, 'and this is our retarded son, Dennis.' It always made me feel so bad." Dennis sobbed uncontrollably as the years of heartbreak washed over him again.

Amy tried to comfort him. She explained that years ago many people thought sharing this information as Dennis's dad did was OK. Perhaps they thought people with disabilities didn't really understand. "So you see," Amy consoled, "they didn't know their words would hurt."

But Dennis understood, and that label cut to the core. After decades, Dennis still heard: *"My son is retarded."*

> Labels can cut to the core.

We all have labels in our thought closets we wish weren't there. Some we place on ourselves, like *idiot* or whatever name you call yourself. Labels hurt, don't they? Some labels don't originate with us, though. Like Dennis, we receive labels from someone else. Think about the labels in your thought closet.

Write your top three most hurtful, destructive labels:

Circle where those hurtful or untrue labels came from:

**parent   disability   myself   spouse   sibling
employer   physical characteristics   former failures
childhood comments   other** _____

How do your labels make you feel?

Are the labels you wear based on truth? ○ **yes   ** ○ **no**

Dennis may struggle with an intellectual disability, but he understands the word that became a hurtful label. If you have been labeled with unfortunate words, you know how those words can have a hold on you. Destructive, discouraging, or untrue tags come from a definitive source.

Where do lies originate (John 8:44)?
○ **human depravity   ** ○ **social ills   ** ○ **father of lies**
○ **our deceitful hearts   ** ○ **soap operas**

Wearing a discouraging or untruthful label feels like you're in a constant wrestling match. It grabs hold of you, and you struggle against its choke hold. On and on the fight wages.

Often we transfer anger from the painful label to the one who stuck it on us. You may harbor anger toward yourself or someone in your life who said hurtful things. Remind yourself that Satan is the father of lies, and each lie is his offspring.

According to Ephesians 6:12, we do not wrestle against

_____.

We do wrestle against_____.

The ultimate battle is against the Enemy of your soul. People, and even you, inflict some real damage with words. But we give Satan the greatest weapons he uses against us: *bitterness and unforgiveness.* Pause and ask God if you would benefit from forgiving someone ... or yourself? If so, please deal with this. Call one of your Bible-study buddies to pray with you, to help you become accountable to truth and get free!

The Enemy tells lies and tries to stick his lying-labels on you. Do you realize a label only becomes yours if you allow it? If you invite a lie into your thought closet and give it shelf space, it is yours. If you refuse to let it in to stick, it can't brand you! You can begin now to refuse hurtful labels.

Read 2 Corinthians 10:4-5 and learn these steps ...

STEP 1. Crush the lie—demolish every thought opposed to God. How are your labels in opposition to God?

Crush

Write on these labels the lies you have stored in your thought closet. Then, with your blackest marker, draw demolition balls on each one!

Can you imagine each lie crushed as you color? Hmmm ... now you probably can't see the lie anymore. Take a mental picture of this, because I want you to see it the next time a lying-label starts to stick to you. Crush it, blot it out!

Capture

STEP 2. Capture the thought—hold thoughts captive. Write again the lies on your labels. This time draw prison bars on each label!

You hold those lies captive because they've broken God's law. This prisoner is not afforded any rights; it's not subject to the Geneva Convention! It is a convict! No parole! And, it doesn't get a life sentence, it gets the death penalty! Friend, what I'm trying to say is, *keep* that lie imprisoned. Next time you feel it start to squirm, next time it bangs on the prison bars, remind your Enemy that he has no freedom to label you any longer.

**What three things does God give you to maintain victory over the imprisoned lie (2 Tim. 1:7)?
I have:**

Concur

STEP 3. Concur with truth—make them obey Christ. This is where you stick a truthful label over the lie! Read through the truthful labels below. Check which truths you need to cover the lies you've been wearing.

TRUTHFUL LABELS
○ I am a new creation (2 Cor. 5:17).
○ I am forgiven (Eph. 1:7-8).
○ I am gifted with power, love, and a sound mind (2 Tim. 1:7).
○ I am chosen to be fruitful (John 15:16).
○ I am complete (Col. 2:9-10).
○ I am secure (Rom. 8:31-39).
○ I am confident (Phil. 1:6).
○ I am free (Rom. 6:18; 8:1).
○ I am capable (Phil. 4:13).
○ I am spiritually alive (Eph. 2:5).
○ I am God's workmanship (Eph. 2:10).
○ I am welcome in God's presence (Eph. 2:18; Heb. 4:14-16).
○ I am sheltered and protected in God (Col. 3:3).
○ I am valuable to God (1 Cor. 6:20).
○ I am a member of God's family (1 John 3:1-2; Eph. 2:19).
○ I am God's treasure.(1 Pet. 2:9-10).
○ I am dearly loved (Col. 3:12).
○ I am being transformed (2 Cor. 3:18).
○ I am an heir of God (Rom. 8:17).
○ I am a friend of God (John 15:15).
○ I am God's delight (Zeph. 3:17).
○ I am welcomed to draw near to God (Eph. 3:12).

The labels you wear must be truthful. You must tell yourself the truth about who you are no matter what anyone else says. Your Father, God, wants to be the Label Maker for your life.

Ask God to help you receive His labels and reject other labels. As you go through your day, ponder the three "Cs" … Crush, Capture, and Concur!

Day 2
UNCHANGEABLE LABELS: FACT AND FAITH

Yesterday we discussed how labels can have a hold on us. We saw that sometimes we label ourselves, and sometimes others label us. But some labels just come with your life—they are just facts such as *infertile, learning disabled, stay-at-home mom, wife, diabetic, widowed, abused, divorced,* or *blind.*

> Some labels are just facts.

Write your *fact* labels here:

Honestly, I used to try and hide my *blind* label. It seemed my blindness was all people saw. I felt it reduced me to a curiosity and blocked real connection. My friend, labels do that! They mark us by someone else's perception. They impose a barrier that keeps us from connecting with others in an authentic way—if we let them. Do you relate?

Describe a time when you experienced a disconnect because of labels.

Sometimes we self-impose a disconnect. We assign a meaning to our unchangeable label that is far worse than the label itself. We assign a *fate* rather than *faith* to our fact.

For me, blind is my unchangeable label. But if I assign meaning to it that says: "You are different from everyone who is sighted," or "People think you are a burden," or "People feel

> We sometimes assign a fate to our label that is worse than the fact itself.

sorry for you," then what I say to my soul becomes far worse than the label itself. The fate label I wear is worse than the fact. If I do that, I use my label as a foundation to speak lies.

Do you do that? Suppose your fact label is *divorced.* If you assign a fateful meaning such as *rejected* or *unlovable,* then you experience something far worse than the fact itself.

On the labels at left, write the fate you or someone else may have assigned to your *fact* label.

Labels identify us far more than we can imagine. Do you feel your *fate* label is communicating to others as you interact with them?   ○ yes   ○ no

Explain why and how or why not.

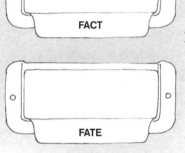

Naomi wore labels and assigned a fate to her fact label.

Look up Ruth 1:20-21. How did Naomi label herself?

Was Naomi's self-imposed label fact, fate, or faith? Why?

Naomi's fact or unchangeable label was *widow.* Based on her perception that God had dealt bitterly with her, she obviously said untruths to her soul that caused her to mislabel herself. It was as if she chose her own fate.

What was Naomi's truthful *faith* label (Ruth 4:14-15)?

God hasn't left you without a redeemer today. He is a Restorer of Life and your Sustainer in old age. Naomi showed up in Bethlehem wearing her fateful label, "dealt bitterly with by God," but it wasn't true. She wore the garment of gloom based on her self-imposed label. The faith label she should have worn was "favored by God."

Naomi wore a hurtful, untruthful label based on her struggle. By the end of the story we see that God defied her self-imposed label. He had not dealt bitterly with her. He showed her great favor by placing her much loved daughter-in-law in the lineage of Christ.

Name Naomi's and Ruth's grandchildren (Ruth 4:22).

Who was referred to as the "root of Jesse" (Isa. 11:10; Rom. 15:12) and "Son of David" (Matt. 1:1; 21:9; 22:42)?

Those beautiful names of Jesus reflect God's favor. Naomi was positioned for ultimate favor, but she wasted her emotions on assuming the worst about her circumstance and God. Had she focused on faith rather than fact, she would have worn a hopeful label. Even our factual labels can still be faith labels.

Hebrews 11:1 says faith labels are based on _____

Personalize this verse for your fact label. What are the things "not seen" or "hoped for"?

We are to wear faith labels and to speak statements of faith to our soul no matter our circumstance—no matter the fact. Naomi could have said to herself, "Naomi, woman of God … you are a widow now. You have no sons to take care of you. You, my dear, now have the amazing opportunity to have the God of your Fathers, the Lord Jehovah, provide for you and protect you. He is the Husband of your people Israel, and He will bring sweetness to your life." She could have said those words to her soul and worn the faith label "favored by God." Instead, she saw the label "widow" and decided to tell her soul her name was "Bitterness."

> We are to wear faith labels and to speak statements of faith.

Do you talk to your soul that way?   ○ yes   ○ no

Which response best fits how your self-talk about your fact label affects your faith?
○ **bolsters it**   ○ **weakens it**   ○ **doesn't affect it**
○ **challenges it**   ○ **hinders it**   ○ **destroys it**

Explain why you chose that response:

My fact is blind. I could interpret that as handicapped (fate) or handicapable (faith)! I could decide blind means disabled or determined! I could assume it means stricken by God (fate) or chosen by God (faith). It is up to you, my friend. You can't change the fact label in your life. What you can change is what you say to your soul about that fact. What you say about that fact is based on your faith in God. If He says you are more than a conqueror, then that's the faith label you wear!

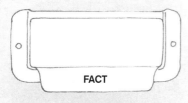

Examine your labels. Do they really represent faith? Or are you like Naomi? Fill in your _faith_ labels at left.

Have you mislabeled yourself because of life's unchangeable label(s)? If so, confess to God and ask Him right now to help you elevate faith over fact. Don't let your own interpretation of your facts keep you from faith.

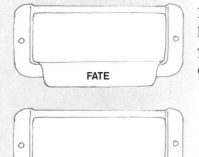

What is the nature of your "seen" fact (2 Cor. 4:18)?

Hebrews 11:1 says faith is the evidence of that which is "not seen." So, wear the faith label and fix your eyes on the unseen; it gives you eternal perspective. Your fact label is temporary! Thank You, Lord!

Talk to yourself today about the real fact label you wear … "dearly loved by God" (and Jennifer)!

Day 3
IT'S A WOMAN'S PREROGATIVE TO CHANGE HER MIND.

Well, hello, my faith-labeled friend! I trust you spoke truth to your soul yesterday and you're wearing what God says about you. Now pour yourself a cup of tea and imagine taking a walk with your best girlfriend. You spot a wad of fabric near a trash can. As you approach, the stench accosts you! Even so, you pick up the nasty fabric and discover it's a woman's blouse.

Hmm, you think, *I wear blouses! I wouldn't have chosen this one, but here it is ...* So you hang it by your favorite jeans and think, *I don't like this, but it's here, so I guess I'll keep it.* Now the whole closet reeks and your clean, lovely clothes get dirty as you shove it in place. It has no value; but now it's yours.

Unlike clothes we don't wear, everything from our thought closets gets worn. Uck! We put on untrue, fateful, hurtful labels. When we allow them in, we take dirty, ill-fitting words and store them in the sanctity of our minds! We must continue to crush those wrong thoughts, capture those lying words, and make each word and label concur with truth because we are to have a particular mind (Phil. 2:5).

Your thought closet is designed to host the mind of Christ. That's why you can't let it become cluttered with wrong words and ill-fitting labels.

> Let this mind be in you, which was also in Christ Jesus.
> Philippians 2:5, KJV

Look at the word *mind* in the following activity, and write words that describe the mind of Christ. I've put in some Scripture hints if you need them.

M (Ps. 8:1; 103:8; Matt. 11:29)

I (Luke 23:4; Titus 2:7)

N (Phil. 4:8; Rev. 19:16; Ps. 34:18)

D (2 Tim. 1:7; 2:15)

Do you realize how you described the mind of Christ is the same way you should describe your own mind? Wow. That's why we shouldn't let our minds become polluted.

Put a minus sign beside the qualities you wrote that are lacking in your thought closet.

How does lacking that mind-of-Christ quality cause you to struggle with "stinkin' thinking"?
Because I lack _____ I struggle with _____
Because I lack _____ I struggle with _____
Because I lack _____ I struggle with _____

We are not to be _____ to this world, but _____ by the renewing of our _____. (Rom. 12:2).

Let's renew our minds. Let's think with the mind of Christ. Let's not conform our thinking to the world's thinking but transform our thoughts by infusing them with the truths of Scripture so they will resemble the mind of Christ.

When the world tells you to make your violators pay, the mind of Christ thinks (Eph. 4:32; Luke 17:3-4):

When the world suggests you look out for number one, the mind of Christ thinks (Col. 3:12):

When the world advises you get all you can—buy now and pay later—the mind of Christ thinks (Matt. 5:41-42):

When the world tells you "just do it," the mind of Christ thinks (2 Pet. 1:5-8):

When the world says you can pull yourself up by your own bootstraps, the mind of Christ thinks (Phil. 2:13):

When the world persuades "it's all about you," the mind of Christ thinks (1 Cor. 6:20; Rev. 4:11):

Friend, we can't afford to conform to the world's thinking. Choosing to believe just one stinky thought will pollute our thought closets. Unless biblical thinking fills us, we won't have the mind of Christ. If we don't have the mind of Christ, any lying label will stick! Unless we tell ourselves scriptural truths, we will conform to the world through faulty thinking.

Your life's wardrobe is directly affected by what is in your thought closet. You must "renew" your mind and tidy it up.

The Pharisees were a prominent sect of Jews. The Hebrew name *Pharisee* means "separatists, or the separated ones." It's critical that we guard the sanctity of our minds and maintain clean, pure thought closets so we will be protected from their trap of polluted thought closets.

What do Matthew 15:1-9 and 21:33-46 say about Pharisees?

How did Jesus describe Pharisees (Matt. 23:3-6)?

The Pharisees' original intention may have been to know truth and please God, but their thought closets eventually became so diluted by tradition and polluted by pride that they didn't even recognize truth when they met Christ. That's what happens to us when we are conformed to the world's thinking rather than being transformed by truth renewing our minds.

Draw below the two pictures that Jesus used to describe the Pharisees in Matthew 23:25-28.

Does either of the pictures remind you of your thought closet?   ○ yes   ○ no   Why or why not?

God wants us to have integrity (Ps. 51:6). Do you struggle with the Pharisee phenomenon? I do. I don't mean to, but I slip into cleaning the outside of my cup and neglecting the inside. If some ill-fitting thought, clumsy consideration, lying label, or faulty thinking is in your thought closet, clean it out now! Look at these verses to celebrate the source of your purification.

God purifies you. "He gave Himself for us to redeem us from all lawlessness and to cleanse for Himself a special people, eager to do good works" (Titus 2:14, HCSB).

> Celebrate the source of your purification.

God will purify your conscience. "How much more will the blood of Christ, who through the eternal Spirit offered Himself without blemish to God, cleanse your conscience from dead works to serve the living God?" (Heb. 9:14).

Purifying yourself keeps you from being double minded. James 4:8 says, "Draw near to God and He will draw near to you. Cleanse your hands, you sinners; and purify your hearts, you double-minded."

As you finish your coffee and our study today, let me quote my friend Patsy. She chuckles, "Everyone needs integration therapy." I love that because I have pondered the word *integration* and its opposite—*disintegration*.

Integration means what is in the thought closet and what people observe are the same. To be integrated means not walking the way of the Pharisees. When the person I am on the outside is who I am on the inside, I am integrated. But when there is a difference—a disunity between my *outside me* and my *inside me*—then I am disintegrated. In other words, I fall apart, slowly crumble, break down.

If you feel like you are unraveling, pray today about purifying your thought closet and renewing your mind so you will have truth on the inside and truth on the outside!

Oh, the freedom authenticity brings! To have truth in your thought closet and to clothe yourself in it! Bring it on!

Day 4
FAULTY ASSUMPTIONS

As a little girl, each Sunday we passed a beautiful Catholic church. Stately and ornate, it didn't look like my church at all, and it always caught my gaze. Then came the day when it amazed me beyond words.

As a child I could see well, and colors, architecture, and even signage captured my attention. You'll understand my astonishment when my eyes landed on an ordinary street sign planted in the parking lot of this extraordinary church that read: Angle Parking Only. I was about six and wasn't a great reader, so I thought it said *Angel* Parking Only. I was in awe the Catholics had angels attending. I'd never seen any at my church! And they were so expected they had reserved parking? Only humans attended our services—and the only reserved parking was for our pastor. I do remember my confusion when I noticed celestial beings drove such average cars! *An angel in a '64 Datsun? I would have expected a Rolls Royce!*

Years later I realized my spelling gaffe. It was fun thinking angels parked at the Catholic church, but it was wrong. My wrong thinking came from a faulty assumption. All of our thoughts are based on our assumptions, our beliefs. That's why we must have truthful assumptions.

Faulty assumptions are not harmless accessories we take on and off. They actually become the base of our thoughts and actions. They anchor the wardrobe of our lives. That's why it's very dangerous to assume something is true when it isn't.

Begin to consider your assumptions. Can you see how they influence your thoughts?

> My wrong thinking came from a faulty assumption.

How are assumptions and thoughts connected?

Before I ask about your specific assumptions, sneak a peek into my thought closet, and I'll show you some of mine!

In college I assumed my worth was measured by my performance. As a result, I filled my thought closet with lots of wrong thinking. Thoughts like *no matter how hard you try, you could have done better.* Does that sound like a faulty assumption and wrong thinking to you?

Did you tuck away some faulty assumptions as an older teen or young adult? List three examples.

Faulty assumption:
Faulty assumption:
Faulty assumption:

As a young wife, I brought my share of faulty assumptions into marriage. My thought closet's ill-fitting beliefs clothed me with wrong thinking. Those misguided thoughts grew into unrealistic expectations, and I couldn't understand why Phil didn't get it! How could he be so insensitive?

I entertained thoughts like, *If he really valued me, he would pick up his clothes and lower the toilet seat.* I thought if Phil did something I didn't like, he didn't value my opinion or think it was important. When he handled things differently, I supposed his priorities were out of line. I assumed that it was all about me. Does that sound like a faulty assumption to you?

What faulty assumptions have you held? If you're not married, answer based on a close relationship (parent, child, sibling, friend, boyfriend).

Faulty assumption:
Faulty assumption:
Faulty assumption:

How did one assumption impact your relationship?

Our assumptions affect everything! They impact our relationships, thoughts, and actions. Let's sneak a peek into some Bible characters' thought closets to see their faulty assumptions.

Find the following characters and write their faulty assumptions next to the references.
Martha (John 11:21)
Jezebel (1 Kings 19:1-2)
Rachel (Gen. 30:1)
Job's wife (Job 2:9)

Faulty assumptions always reveal themselves in wrong thinking and result in erroneous action.

Match the same characters with the resulting actions of their faulty assumptions.

Martha	**Threatened to give up hope if she did not get her way**
Jezebel	**Questioned Jesus' motives behind not coming sooner**
Rachel	**Suggested when life is hard, abandon God and take control**
Job's wife	**Exalted her belief in idolatry against God's miracles**

**With which of the characters do you best relate?
Explain why:**

To willingly allow faulty assumptions in our thought closets is risky. It's to engage in presumption. I want you to see something interesting about the words *assume* and *presume.*

How does your dictionary define *assume?*

Now look up the word *presume.* What does it mean?

Those words are quite similar, aren't they? In fact, the Latin root of both words is the same: *-sume,* meaning to take. I wanted you to see the similarity of those two words because Scripture warns against acting with presumption.

Read Psalm 19:13 (NASB). What does the psalmist pray God would keep him from?

> Scripture warns against acting with presumption.

The Hebrew word translated to our English *presumptuous (zed)* in that verse means arrogant, proud, or insolent.

Describe a time you have been presumptuous:

**Was your presumption arrogant or humble?
Was your willingness to presume a result of pride or submission? Explain.**

How does presumption reveal itself according to 2 Peter 2:10?

Does that sound arrogant, proud or insolent to you?
○ **yes** ○ **no**

Reconsider your presumption. Was it fueled by a faulty assumption? ○ yes ○ no If so, describe your faulty assumption and the wrong thinking that resulted:

> Only God's way, view, and opinion are worthy of becoming the foundation of our thought closets.

The Greek word for "presumptuous" in 1 Peter is *tolmetes,* meaning "a daring man." My friend, to engage in assumption is to be presumptuous. It is to be a daring woman in the worst way! It is to take for granted that your way, your view, and your opinion are worthy of forming the foundation of your thoughts. Only God's way, view, and opinion are worthy of becoming the foundation of our thought closets.

Presumption shows itself in me when I wrongly assume my perspective is complete but it is actually limited by my experiences and flawed by my sinful nature. The fact that I act on my presumptions implies in the depth of my heart I trust and prefer my view above God's.

Have you ever been willing to hold on to faulty assumptions as acts of presumption? Explain.

My friend, when God showed me this, I asked Him to forgive me for engaging in presumption. If God is showing you the same, repent of this and ask God for His forgiveness.

Read Psalm 19:13 again aloud as a prayer.

Let's end our time together today by committing the foundation of our thought closets to God's truth, not faulty assumptions. We want thought closets teeming with truth, full of right thinking, and grounded with God's thoughts, not our own.

I want you to memorize Psalm 19:13, so write it on a sticky note or index card and carry it around with you today. Meditate on it and pray it constantly so your thought closet will have God's light shining brightly in it, exposing any faulty assumption in there. Bless you, my sister.

Day 5
ROOTS AND FRUITS

Suppose your spaceship just landed on planet Earth. (Yes, you are now an alien!) The hydraulic door opened, lowered you to terra firma, and plopped you in the middle of a lush plantation. You would certainly be curious about the different varieties of growth you encountered. (Rumor has it aliens are very nosy.) So, how would you satisfy that extraterrestrial inquisitiveness? How would you determine the kind of trees you saw?

As an alien tree examiner, you could certainly dig down to cut a sample from the root system or perhaps take some kind of core section from deep within the living wood. But the most practical way to figure out what kind of tree you were looking at (especially if your alien invasion was on a tight schedule) would be to examine its fruit.

To understand the unseen part of a tree, you study the seen part. Fruit reveals the nature, the life, and the root of a tree. However, the opposite also applies. To understand the seen part of your life, you examine the unseen part. To understand why your life is wardrobed as it is, you must examine the contents and foundation of your thought closet.

Yesterday we looked at faulty assumptions. Faulty assumptions are roots. Wrong thinking is fruit. We saw the assumptions and thoughts of some biblical characters and considered our own. Today we will further examine our assumptions and thoughts. We will check out our roots and taste our fruit! Like that alien root examiner, let's use scriptural principles to guide us.

> Let scriptural principles guide you as you examine your assumptions and thoughts.

PRINCIPLE 1: FRUIT EXPOSES ROOTS

Hebrews 12:15 shows the link between roots and fruit. What does it warn against?

What is the "fruit" that the writer of Hebrews suggests springs from the "root" of bitterness?

The fruits that spring from the root of bitterness are difficulty and corruption. In other words, if you engage in the faulty assumption that bitterness is appropriate for a daughter of Christ, it becomes a root in your life from which the fruit of trouble will sprout. If you invite bitterness into your thought closet, you will wardrobe yourself with troublesome thoughts and destructive emotions.

Stop and ask God to first show you the bitter and sour fruit in your life. What is your fruit? Are you hypersensitive with other people—as I was with Phil? Do you constantly interpret other people's words and actions as personal attacks? Defensive thinking and hypersensitive emotions are fruit.

Here's another fruit. During my college years I was paralyzed by the notion that nothing I did was good enough. That assumption bore the fruit of perfectionism. Do you ever find that fruit in your life? If your fruit of perfectionism has matured, you may place those same unrealistic demands on the people you love.

Draw some fruit in the margin and label them with the result of your faulty assumptions. Underneath each fruit describes it (for example, poison, sour, or nourishing).

You and I don't simply sprout the fruits of insecurity, anger, intolerance, low self-esteem, or defensiveness without something to first feed those feelings or thoughts. Feelings and thoughts are fruits. Assumptions are roots.

PRINCIPLE 2: CHANGING THE FRUIT IS IMPOSSIBLE WITHOUT CHANGING THE ROOT

Roots are powerful and they seem to evidence their DNA even when we don't want them to. We may really dislike the fruit, but it just seems to keep on growing.

My friend, the sour fruit of defensiveness has been one of the most distasteful that has blossomed and left a pungent taste in our marriage. I tried to pray that fruit away. I confessed that fruit as sin and repented. I tried to will it away, and it just seemed to be a die-hard fruit!

How do Hosea 9:16 and Matthew 7:17-18 reveal the relationship of roots and fruit?

We can't will our fruits from blossoming. There is only one way to deal with bad-tasting fruit, and that is to kill the root. A fruit can't be nourished if there is no root. Rather than growing frustrated over the discouraging nature of our fruit, we can be encouraged to recognize that our fruit will die if the root dies.

When I reacted with hypersensitivity or defensiveness to Phil, I learned to check the root. Was I operating out of a faulty assumption? My answer was usually yes. Phil wasn't devaluing me in a moment of messiness or forgetfulness. His thoughts weren't even about me when he left the toilet seat up. (I guess I'm glad for that on some level.)

> **Choose one of the fruits you drew and describe what triggers that thought, reaction, or feeling:**

> **What underlying assumption feeds that thought or feeling?**

What you just wrote is a root. Keep that in mind.

PRINCIPLE 3: BAD FRUIT DOESN'T GROW FROM GOOD ROOTS

My fruit of defensiveness grew from the root of pride and insecurity. My assumption was, "I can't afford to be wrong. My value depends on being right," or "My opinion is right because it's mine!" Now it's your turn.

> **Draw roots under the fruit you drew. On each root write the faulty assumption from which they have grown.**

The fruit of hypersensitivity grows from the root of pride and an unhealthy level of self-consciousness. The fruit of perfectionism springs from the root of low self-esteem or insecurity. You get the idea. Look at the roots you just drew. Each root is most likely a faulty assumption.

> **On what underlying assumption did the children of Israel operate (Deut. 1:27)?**

51

The fruit of that faulty assumption is clear. What fruit did they display (result of that root) in verse 26?

Their root was a faulty assumption about the character and purposes of God. Hence, the fruit of wrong thinking sprouted in the form of discounting God's command and rebelling.

Moses tried to sprinkle truth on their poisonous root. What did he tell them in Deuteronomy 1:29,31?

If the Hebrew people had vibrant roots of truth in their thought closets, they would have tasted healthy fruit. If they had not acted presumptuously but rather believed God and accepted truth that says, "God will fight for us; I won't be afraid," they would have produced the fruit of confidence and obedience from the root of faith and security.

Deuteronomy 1:32 reveals the true nature of and cause of faulty assumptions. According to this verse, circle the reason we accept faulty assumptions.

Insecurity   Fear   Pride   Unbelief   Carelessness

My friend, unbelief feeds faulty assumptions. Not believing God fertilizes that root leads you to further presumption.

Examine the roots you drew and labeled. How do those roots reflect unbelief?

The weapon of the Word kills bad roots. Just as we have talked about speaking truth to our souls and crushing lies, we do the same to our roots. We confront those assumptions with truth. Each time you taste a bitter fruit, trace the root. When you find the root to be faulty, cut it off with the sword of the Spirit.

How does 2 Corinthians 10:4 describe your weapon?

Your weapon is not your will or your feelings; your weapon is God's truth. When your assumptions raise themselves up against the knowledge of God, wield your sword! Cut off the root so it cannot bear fruit! Ask God to strengthen your belief in Him and equip you to do battle using His Word against the faulty assumptions in your thought closet. Confess to God truthful beliefs in prayer.

Dear God,

I believe You are:

I believe:

I believe:

I believe:

Help my unbelief (Mark 9:24). Amen.

My sister, once some of those nasty roots are choked out of your thought closet by the weapon of truth, you will be clothed with the lovely fruit God intended. You will have more room in your thought closet for the life-giving roots to grow strong. Our good fruit is ultimately from the root of Christ and His Spirit in us (Phil. 1:11; Gal. 5:22-23). Next week we will learn how God's Spirit helps us control our thought closets and how the wisdom of Christ can be the watchman at the closet door. Until then, mind your labeling, keep the inside of your thought closet pure, and monitor your assumptions, for as a woman "thinketh," so is she (Prov. 23:7, KJV)! Good work!

> Our good fruit is ultimately from the root of Christ and His Spirit in us.

session two

LISTENING GUIDE

Some of us would rather be _____-_____ than risk-takers.

The first two servants or risk-takers _____ or
_____ their talents.

The third servant went away and _____ his talent.

The third servant is a _____-_____.

The hole-maker (servant) did not have a _____
_____ of his master.

Hole-makers do not experience life and growth.
They cling to their _____ _____.

CONVERSATION GUIDE
1. Share with the group your faith/fact labels.
2. Why do you think we cling to our shovels (faulty assumptions) rather than cling to truth?

Video sessions are available for download at *www.lifeway.com/women*

week
THREE

A WISE THOUGHT CLOSET

The wisdom from above is first pure, then peaceable, gentle, reasonable, full of mercy and good fruits, unwavering, without hypocrisy.

JAMES 3:17, NASB

Sneak a peek into Kathy Troccoli's thought closet ...

I love to be around Kathy! She's Italian, got a thick New York accent and is a gifted singer/songwriter who communicates warmth and depth as she speaks, sings, and writes books. She's a woman with an issue of ... wisdom!

"I used to think too much with my feelings. When I was bulimic for 10 years, I'd feel "you'll never get well" or "you'll never be able to get out of this." But God says, "I am a Healer" and "In Me you are more than a conqueror."

"Many women deal with self-esteem issues: 'I'm not good enough.' Or, 'I don't think God really forgives me.' What happens is they rely on those lies and they bring them down; but there's wisdom in the truth of God, wisdom in His promises. As I've confronted my issues and feelings with truth, I've become wiser. I'm now able to take what I've learned from not being pushed by feelings but instead holding onto truth, and it's made me stronger. I hear it coming out of my mouth as wisdom. I feel like I'm wise in ways I couldn't have been before when I was drowning beneath big waves of emotion."

To read more from Kathy, check out *Selftalksoultalk.com.*

Day 1
THE WATCHMAN AT YOUR THOUGHT-CLOSET DOOR

Have you ever awakened from a bad dream and been mad because someone in your dream upset you? You feel sad, irritated, or worried. After time and strong coffee, the morning brain fog lifts and you realize it was all in your mind. But it felt so real. That's a tiny picture of what living out a false assumption is like. It feels real, but it's not true.

Feelings are powerful, but they don't always represent truth. When we wake from a bad dream, we have to adjust our feelings to truth rather than keep following the fiction of our prior slumber. In a far more difficult arena but with the same principle, we must take control of what we say to our souls— make our inner speech truth driven rather than feeling driven.

> **Think of a time your emotions got out of control. What kinds of thoughts or actions resulted?**
>
> **Emotion:**
>
> **Thought:**
>
> **Action:**

We have two choices concerning our thought closet contents: Act according to truth or react to our emotions. Our thought closets have room for both. Feelings are valid, but they must concur with truth to be worthy of our life's wardrobe! We need to understand the basic nature of our feelings so we can give emotions their proper placement.

> **According to Jeremiah 17:9, can our hearts (feelings), be fully trusted? ○ yes ○ no**

If you think with your feelings, you can fall into all manner of false conclusions. Feelings are supposed to serve and strengthen us. Left to themselves, however, they enslave and deplete us.

> **Ask the Holy Spirit to give you some insight as you consider these two questions.**
>
> **In what ways do I think with my feelings?**
>
> **Do my feelings serve me well or am I their slave?**

Through the gift of wisdom God protects us against the self-deceit and enslavement that come from thinking with our feelings. So, before we grab a bin of wisdom and throw it into our thought closets, we must determine what kind we need.

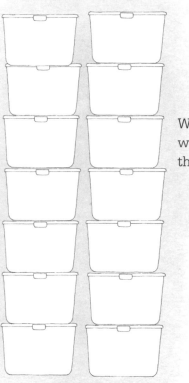

Write on the first stack of bins at left what God's wisdom is like (Jas. 3:17). On the second, list the opposite of each.

Circle attributes you lack in the first stack. What erosive emotions keep you from those wise qualities?

Without God's wisdom, we stumble in our reasoning, think with our feelings, and accept lies for truth. Just what does thinking with our feelings look like?

Describe how these characters showed lack of wisdom.

Esau (Gen. 25:29-34)

David (2 Sam. 11:1-5,14-17)

Sarah (Gen. 16:1-6)

What emotions caused each of them to act unwisely?

> A surplus of emotion usually precedes acting without wisdom.

A surplus of emotion usually precedes acting without wisdom. Read that again—I don't want you to pass over it too quickly! When we operate out of human wisdom or don't realize we lack God's wisdom, we think and act according to our feelings.

Think of a time you lacked wisdom. What feelings preceded your unwise act?

Since feelings are powerful, our thought closets must be full of wisdom. Wisdom is the watchman at your thought-closet door. Without its protection, untruth can sneak in when it feels true.

So how do we get a big bin of God's wisdom (Prov. 2:6; Jas. 1:5)?

○ **Beg for it**   ○ **Request it**   ○ **Barter for it**   ○ **Earn it**
○ **Inherit it**   ○ **Receive it**   ○ **Acquire it before senility**

Simply ask God for wisdom; He gives wisdom.

Have you ever asked God for wisdom? Describe a time you asked and the result of your request. If you have never asked, put your request in writing:

I remember when I first petitioned God for wisdom when I was only 13 years old. Since then, I constantly ask. And God consistently gives. Wisdom is more reliable than feelings. It will set off little alarms to alert you to the impending enemy invader. Imagine if the wisdom-lacking people we've just studied hadn't thought with their feelings at the moment of their emotionally-charged crisis point.

Write below next to their names what the potential outcome could have been if they had pulled from the "Wisdom Bin" in their thought closets.

Esau:

Esau became a nation called Edom, which remained one of Israel's greatest enemies and consequently experienced God's judgment. God stated Edom would never be rebuilt. Just as Edom had perpetual hatred for Israel, their country would remain perpetually empty. Various countries have controlled the territory that was once Edom, but Edom as a nation disappeared. What a sad result of an emotionally charged, wisdom-lacking initial act (Num. 20:14-21; Jer. 49:17).

David:

The actual result of David's feeling-driven thoughts and actions were guilt, adultery, murder, the death of his child, and family strife. Oh, how wisdom would have protected him from heartbreak and regret (2 Sam. 12:5-7,10-11,15-18).

Sarah:

Because Sarah thought with her feelings, she didn't wait on God's timing. The result was Ishmael, the son of her maidservant, Hagar. Although he became a great nation (Gen. 17:20), he was at odds with his brothers (16:12). Muslims consider themselves children of Ishmael, so the conflict continues today.

Without wisdom we act emotionally, think with our feelings, and don't recognize truth—with catastrophic results. Why would we babble reckless words to ourselves based on our feelings when Christ offers wisdom just for the asking?

As you tune into your inner chatter today, ask, *"Is what I'm saying wise and true?" "Am I thinking with feelings?" "Do my feelings serve me well right now, or am I being enslaved?"* If your answers aren't satisfactory, ask God for wisdom.

Remember, God has placed you in a group with others who seek to grow. Perhaps your call to a Bible study buddy to ask her to pray with you about this or to help you monitor your feelings will actually help her become wiser too. Bless you.

Day 2
MORE WAYS TO FILL YOUR THOUGHT CLOSET WITH WISDOM

I know some of our days of study have required a double shot, fully loaded, venti-size coffee! And I know some days have left you worn out from digging deep into your thought closet and Scripture. Today you can pour an herbal tea or a decaf and relax! We will explore two more ways to receive wisdom, and they will delight and encourage you. Yesterday, we learned about the primary way to receive wisdom—ask for it.

Now look in Proverbs 9:10 and write the second way you can receive the wisdom you need.

What do you think it means to fear God?

In the following paragraph underline key descriptions of the meaning of fearing God.

To fear the Lord means we revere Him and show deference and respect. It's acting toward God as if approaching a king who invited us into his royal chamber We are keenly aware of God's high position and the honor of approaching Him! To fear God means we esteem His truth more highly than our feelings or perceptions of truth. To fear the Lord means holding His knowledge and truth in higher regard than our own.

Hebrew scribes meticulously copied the text of the Old Testament to preserve Scripture for future generations, and they wrote the name of God countless times. The consonants "YHWH" denote His holy name. Biblical scholars are not sure what the vowels are for the divine name of God known today as the *tetragrammaton*. "Yahweh" is our closest guess.

Before a Masoretic scribe would write the name of God, he would first wash himself and then use a new pen. This was to show respect for the name of God and to carefully keep from breaking the Third Commandment (Ex. 20:7).

A Jew never uttered the name of God when reading Scripture aloud out of fear of the Lord. Instead, he would substitute "Adonai," which means "Lord" or "Master." This may be the reason the disciple Matthew most often used the phrase "kingdom of heaven" instead of "kingdom of God."

Now, don't misunderstand. Faithful men and women throughout the Bible spoke the name of God. God is our Father,

> Masoretes were Jewish scribes who copied the Old Testament text before the invention of the printing press.

and we should speak His name. But we should do so with fear or reverence—never casually or crassly. We could all benefit from having a little of the Jewish people's fear factor.

We should guard ourselves against using God's name without respect or "in vain," as the Third Commandment says. "God" is not a stand-in for "Wow!" So how about your fear factor? Think about how you regard and revere God. Check out the questions below and do a self-assessment.

Examine your own heart and mind. My friend, do you fear the Lord? ○ **yes** ○ **no**

Whose truth do you elevate most highly—yours, our culture's, or God's?   Why?

Measure your "fear of the Lord" by the way you answer the following questions.

1. **Do you say the name of God casually? For example, "Oh Lord!" or "Oh my God!"**
   ○ **never** ○ **sometimes** ○ **often** ○ **always**
2. **How do you feel when you hear someone say God's name as profanity?**
   ○ **don't notice** ○ **doesn't bother me**
   ○ **bothers me a little** ○ **bothers me a lot**
   ○ **breaks my heart**
3. **Do you consider your clothes an act of worship?**
   ○ **never think about it** ○ **sometimes**
   ○ **depends on the place I'm going** ○ **always**
4. **What times or places do you consider sacred?**
   ○ **church only** ○ **Christian gatherings only**
   ○ **patriotic events only** ○ **everywhere**
5. **Does your conversation reflect reverence for God?**
   ○ **never** ○ **sometimes** ○ **often** ○ **always**
6. **Do your entertainment selections reveal that all of life is sacred?**
   ○ **never** ○ **sometimes** ○ **often** ○ **always**
7. **Does your life demonstrate the character of God?**
   ○ **never** ○ **sometimes** ○ **often** ○ **always**

**Notice how you responded to the questions above.
Are you satisfied with the answers you checked?
Ask God to lead you to repentance and/or greater
dependence on Him concerning the areas where
you lack reverence for Him.**

Until you revere God most highly in your life, you will never
find true wisdom.

Whew! OK, maybe that was not so decaf, but this will
be! The third way to receive wisdom is to *receive counsel.*

Once again, the Book of Proverbs advises us that
"wisdom is with those who receive counsel," and "a wise man
is he who listens to counsel" (Prov. 13:10; 12:15). When we
walk with wisdom, it will wear off on us.

Often we need to take time to listen to others, learn from
their mistakes and experiences, and recognize they struggle
too. That's why each week begins with a peek into another
woman's thought closet. They can become wise guides in
our lives. Do you have a wise guide (and it should be a female
unless it's your husband, father, or brother)?

> When we walk
> with wisdom, it will
> wear off on us.

**Describe your wise guide or the woman you will ask
God to bring into your life to serve in this capacity.**

How does she encourage wisdom in your life?

Maybe you are a wise guide. You have received wisdom from
God and you reverence Him. You will keep growing in wisdom
as you continue to or begin to give.

**Do you know someone to whom you can/should impart
God's wisdom? If so, who?**

**Ask God what you should do about the person He laid
on your heart.**

You will become well-acquainted with wisdom when you
simply request it, revere God, and receive wise counsel.

When you do, wisdom will not only be the watchman at your thought-closet door, but it will become one of your best friends.

Say to wisdom, "You are my sister." *And call understanding your intimate friend* (Prov. 7:4, emphasis added).

I love that. If wisdom were truly your sister, what would she say to you on a casual morning walk along the river? If understanding actually happened to be your best and most intimate friend, what would she say to you in earnest conversation at a corner table in your favorite café?

You can count on one thing. You wouldn't want to miss a single word. So invite her into your thought closet by requesting, revering God, and receiving counsel.

My friend, remember these three Rs to wisdom: *Request it, Revere God, and Receive counsel.* As you apply yourself to wisdom, your thought closet will be well-guarded, and you will be clothed with truth. Oh, you look marvelous!

> Three Rs
> to wisdom:
> Request it,
> Revere God, and
> Receive counsel.

Day 3
SPEAKING TRUTH TO YOUR ISSUES

I don't know her name, but she had a thought closet full of wisdom. Mark 5 gives us access to it, and after a quick peek, I'm convinced she, you, and I have a lot in common.

First of all, the woman talked to herself. I like her already. And second, she had issues!

I've got issues, you've got issues, all God's children got issues! Issues like illness, financial troubles, insecurities, relationship conflict, fear, and sadness. Our thought closets are jammed with tricky stuff.

What kinds of issues are crowding your thought closet?

Let's get to know this woman in Mark 5. What was her primary issue (Mark 5:25)?

This woman had a single, insurmountable issue, and she had endured it for 12 long years. It had challenged her physically, strained her emotionally, drained her financially, and ostracized her socially.

Which of her descriptions best expresses the result of your issue?

Why?

Her "issue of blood" (KJV) created a load of other issues. What were they (Mark 5:26; see also Lev. 15:25)?

We often face one defining circumstance that becomes the headwater from which other issues flow. The issue of being overweight, for instance, can lead to low self-esteem, shaky confidence, and poor health. Maybe you grew up hearing and believing messages such as "You aren't good at anything," or "You were an accident." If you've endured defining words like those, you may battle with issues of self-worth or depression.

For me, blindness is a big issue that opens the door to a host of others. Some of the biggest daily stressors I face are not being able to drive, read, or enjoy independence. And stress, as you know, can morph itself into monster issues such as anger, isolation, or identity crisis. Our issues come with accessories that take up room in our thought closets!

What complications result from your primary issue?

So what are we to do? Is a steady conversation of wise and truthful self-talk enough to remedy our issues? No, a time comes when you must speak a word to your soul that prompts action resulting in healing.

What did the issue-laden woman do in Mark 5:27?

What did she say to herself in Mark 5:28?

There it is: *She talked to herself.* She confronted her issue and practiced some soul talk. (And she hadn't even done this study!) She told herself if she touched Jesus, she would be healed. She encouraged, counseled, and advised her soul.

Her wise words prompted her action. She extended her arm through the middle of a crowd to touch her fingers to the hem of Jesus' robe. With that brush of homespun cloth across her fingertips, her great need ran head-on into His limitless provision. In that instant, her courage met His compassion. Her hope met His holiness.

What does Mark 5:29 tell us about her encounter with Christ?

Few biblical stories validate my own soul talk more than this story about a hurting woman. Psychologists might say she was merely an example of the power of positive self-talk, but that's an incomplete rendering at best and an untrue conclusion at worst. The most important thing isn't that she talked to herself. It's what she told herself that matters. She didn't mouth a bunch of happy talk or feel-good phrases. She spoke words of wisdom and truth to her soul.

Counseling ourselves to act on truth and coaching ourselves on to make good choices are healthy and wise. Wise soul talk helps us overcome our issues. The woman with the hemorrhage clearly benefited by telling herself she would be healed if she touched Jesus' robe.

What brought her healing (Mark 5:30-34)?
her tenacity   her self-talk   her faith   her desperation

Now, my friend, what I am about to say next is one of the most important statements of our study. Let these words sink in.

Jesus never said her soul talk made her well. He said it was her *faith.* Her *faith* invited healing. Her soul talk contributed to her faith, but it didn't replace her faith. She spoke truth to her soul in the same way you and I need to speak truth to our souls. By faith we receive truth. By faith we believe truth. And by faith we act on truth.

Soul talk can never substitute for faith. The woman could

never have talked herself into healing—not in a hundred years. But she did talk herself into seeking Jesus, and that was what she needed. Soul talk is faith's companion, not its replacement.

Our issues can dictate our beliefs, color our actions, and affect our attitudes, but so can our faith. It's essential we have a thought closet full of wisdom and center our soul talk on the truth of Scripture and on our faith in Christ.

Now, lean back, relax, and end our day with this story.

Once upon a time, in a faraway land, there was a desperately unhappy woman who talked to herself.

She might have said any number of things. She might have told herself to cheer up, to walk on the sunny side of the street, to whistle while she worked, or to simply accept her lot in life. She might even have told herself that her problems were illusions; she was really healthy and whole.

But those aren't the sort of things she said when she spoke to her soul. What she *did* say led her to an act of faith more daring than anything she could have imagined. When this woman talked to herself, it initiated an encounter that brought immediate healing to her body and soul. It was all because of what she had in her thought closet during one of the most important conversations of her life. She told herself the truth, and that led her straight to Jesus. May you be that woman.

Day 4

A SPIRIT-CONTROLLED THOUGHT CLOSET: SNAPSHOTS OF THE SPIRIT

My friend, today I want you to settle in a cozy chair with your Bible and see some word pictures. These snapshots will show how the Holy Spirit can help you deal with your issues and keep control in your thought closet. When we receive Christ, we receive His Spirit (Eph. 1:13-14; 1 Cor. 3:16).

> Soul talk is faith's companion, not its replacement.

How does Jesus identify the Holy Spirit (John 15:26; 16:7)?

Jesus identified the Holy Spirit as a Helper (NASB). The Greek word used is *parakletos (paraclete).* The apostle John recorded Jesus' using the word four times to classify the Holy Spirit's work. *Paraclete* carries an assortment of meanings: Advocate, Defender, Helper, Comforter, and Counselor.

List the activities of the Holy Spirit in believers as revealed in the following verses.

John 14:16
John 14:26
John 16:13

> The Holy Spirit is Advocate, Defender, Helper, Comforter, and Counselor, a representative of Christ, a Teacher, and the One who reminds us of truth.

The Holy Spirit is a Counselor, a representative of Christ, a Teacher, and the One who remind us of truth. So what does that look like? How does God's Spirit help guide and control our soul talk? Today we will look at two snapshots of the Spirit, and tomorrow we will look at two more. As you read, ask God to reveal truth to you, and be ready to jot your thoughts and questions in the margins.

SNAPSHOT 1: GOD'S SPIRIT COUNSELS US

As Phil and I prepared to celebrate our fifth anniversary, we concluded we didn't need celebration; we needed counseling. We fought about the same things all the time, though neither of us was ever wrong!

We loved each other but we didn't like each other much. So with our pride pushed aside, off to counseling we went.

After months of hearing, admitting, and embracing truth, we had a stronger, happier marriage. We not only loved each other but finally liked each other again. Larry, our counselor, was wise and objective. He listened and made us think. He was safe and committed to our good, so we trusted him.

All of us need a counselor from time to time, and the Holy Spirit is the perfect Counselor. He is safe, wise, objective, and absolutely committed to your ultimate good. My friend, you can trust Him never to lead you off course.

Which of the preceding qualities of the Holy Spirit mean the most to you right now and why?

God's Spirit challenges us to hear, admit, and embrace truth.

Which action do you most need in your thought closet?
hear truth   admit truth   embrace truth

Ask God's Spirit to empower you to commit to that.

The Holy Spirit will not shout down the noise of our busy world to counsel you. He won't try to silence all the racket in your thought closet to be heard. To hear His counsel, we have to quiet ourselves and truly *listen*.

I know sometimes when I hear His gentle voice counsel me I am hesitant. I can't always distinguish His voice from my own thoughts and intuition. Do you ever feel that same uncertainty? When we are walking with Christ, though, I believe God's Spirit speaks to us more than we realize. He counsels us through the words of Scripture and the remarks of others.

Can you think of a time when you received counsel from the Holy Spirit? If so, describe it:

If you aren't aware of His counsel, ask God to reveal the Holy Spirit's work in your life, and commit to listening for His voice.

What God has shown me about this role of His Spirit:

How I will act according to the truth He showed me:

SNAPSHOT 2: GOD'S SPIRIT REPRESENTS CHRIST

As a junior at Palm Beach Atlantic University, I joined the Ambassadors who represented our institution at community events. I never imagined I would end up at the exclusive Breakers Hotel in posh Palm Beach at an international gala ... greeting none other than the Princess of Wales!

The contributing philanthropist asked our school to provide students to help at the gala. So in a borrowed evening gown, I arrived with my fellow starstruck coeds. My job was to welcome guests, ask them whether they were patrons or bene-factors, and direct them to the proper dining room.

I knew this was important because of how our advisor coached us (OK, threatened us). We were told our actions would directly reflect on the university. Our duty was to represent the college well. I also figured out how big of a deal this was when security cordoned off the entryway—and the paparazzi crowded behind my partner, Jamie, and me.

The guests arrived—Bob Hope, Victor Borge, Merv Griffin. Then a hush fell. There she was. The princess.

Jamie provided colorful commentary as the much-loved royal shyly lowered her head and walked through the door to cheers and flashing cameras. Princess Diana sauntered past in her dazzling fuchsia gown, and security whisked her away.

I was mindful I represented my university. Even if I wanted to scream, "Diana, I love you! Can I borrow your dress?" or though I may have wished to foxtrot with Bob Hope in his tux and tennis shoes, I would not because my role was to represent the character of my college.

> The Holy Spirit's guidance always lines up with the truth of God's Word.

The Holy Spirit is God's representative. He mirrors God's truth because He is the third Person of the triune God. If you sense the Spirit leading your thoughts or guiding your actions, His guidance always lines up with the truth of God's Word.

What does 1 John 5:6 disclose about God's Spirit? He is:

The Spirit is the truth and *never* leads us in ways that oppose Scripture. He won't; He can't, because Scripture is truth. He represents and lifts up the person of Jesus. He gives illumina-tion to the character and ways of God.

So when you sense the Spirit is guiding you, use this test: Does this match up with the truth of the Bible?

What is your most problematic self-talk? Ask God's Spirit if it matches Scripture's truth. Write here what He tells you:

Now, if it doesn't match, throw it out of your thought closet and send it packing to the Island of Misfit Thoughts!

Draw an island in the margin and write within it those unworthy thoughts.

Sister, if your thoughts don't concur with Scripture, they're not from the Spirit—and they don't belong in your thought closet.

My response to this role of God's Spirit:

Actions I will take because of this truth:

Ponder those two pictures of the Holy Spirit and be sensitive to His voice in your thought closet. More tomorrow …

Finish our time today by asking God's Spirit to counsel you and reveal who Christ is. Bless you.

Day 5
TWO MORE SNAPSHOTS OF THE SPIRIT

We've seen that God's Spirit counsels us and represents Christ and the truth. Today we'll see how He teaches and reminds us of truth. So pour your tea, grab your Bible, and settle in.

SNAPSHOT 3: GOD'S SPIRIT IS OUR TEACHER
I call my husband "Dr. Phil" partly because he really *is* Dr. Phil—he has his Ph.D. I figure after six years of grad school and getting that dissertation done, he deserves the respect.

It's pretty cool that I have my very own personal Dr. Phil. (Mine isn't the famous therapist with a TV show, but he does have hair!) He's a professor; so with briefcase in hand, he playfully proclaims his motto as he leaves for campus: "Going to stamp out some ignorance."

That's what teachers do. They enlighten and instruct; they replace ignorance with knowledge. God's Spirit performs that same task in our lives. He stamps out ignorance, replacing it with wisdom and discernment light years beyond our own.

The following verses reveal why we need a teacher. Match the verses to lessons we can learn.

Psalm 86:11   **I must be taught good judgment and knowledge.**

Psalm 90:12   **I must learn God's way so I can walk in His truth.**

Psalm 119:33   **I want to learn to do God's will.**

Psalm 119:66   **I need to learn the way of God's statutes.**

Psalm 143:10   **I must learn to number my days so I may get a heart of wisdom.**

The Holy Spirit is a mentor who teaches us to know truth, God, and His ways. That means if you are relying on faulty assumptions, He will reveal the roots to you. He exposes wrong thinking and enlightens us to the truth.

Before I owned an audio Bible, I was able to recall much of its truth. Of course, I read it as a child and listened to countless sermons. But I marvel how I was and am able to know and remember so much Scripture, especially as my eyesight began to fail and my Scripture intake was severely limited several years. I am convinced God's Spirit was my teacher.

My friend, do not tell yourself you're not smart enough, young enough, or studious enough to know and remember God's truth. Stay in the Word, and the Holy Spirit will teach you and remind you of truth. I am so grateful for this role He plays in our lives. Learning from Him is the only way to deal with the issues that threaten to crowd our thought closets. We need a Teacher who stamps out the ignorance that pervades our thoughts and assumptions. We need a mentor who can offer wisdom that reaches beyond our own.

How have you benefited from the Holy Spirit's teaching?

My response to this role of God's Spirit:

Actions I will take based on what I've learned about the Holy Spirit as my teacher:

> We need a mentor who can offer wisdom that reaches beyond our own.

SNAPSHOT 4: GOD'S SPIRIT REMINDS US OF TRUTH

I sat in front of a little girl and her dad. We'd been on the tarmac 45 minutes when the captain pierced our collective irritation. "Folks, we appreciate your patience. Maintenance assures me we should be ready to roll in about 15 minutes."

Fellow passengers groaned, and I agreed. For the past 45 minutes, I'd been compiling a mental list of all the things I didn't like about this particular air carrier. I'd been dwelling on all the bad experiences I'd had in airports lately. *We'll just see,* I thought. *It'll be a miracle if this plane takes off in 15 minutes.* But I really wasn't looking for miracles. From a dark corner in my thought closet I was pulling out things that were ugly, ill-fitting, and making me tense. Those ruminations were interrupted by the little girl in the seat behind me.

"Daddy," she chimed. "I spy something blue." Determined to be cheerful, the father guessed, "Is it that bug?" And so the game went.

"Daddy, I spy something good."

Her dad laughed. I figured he laughed for the same reason I did. It was pretty hard to spy anything good in our caged predicament.

"Is it a bag of M&M®s?" he asked.

"No," his daughter giggled.

"Is it your new shoes or your sweet smile?"

A tenderness washed over me as I eavesdropped. Their words cut through my complaining and frustration and reminded me to fix my thoughts on "something good."

In that moment, I decided to "4:8" my thoughts. That's

Philippians 4:8! Find it in your Bible and review the standards of our meditation.

I began to let my thoughts dwell only on what was true, lovely, and of a good report. I spy something lovely. *Father, I prayed. You have provided opportunities for me. You have opened doors and made my path straight.* I reminded myself delays were simply some of the bumps along the road.

Once I fixed my thoughts on truth, I was able to enjoy the rest of my journey. When I chose to place "praiseworthy" thoughts in my thought closet, the motionless airplane became a sanctuary of peace. My issues of delays and frustration were made easier as I prayed and told myself the truth.

> You can choose to place praiseworthy thoughts in your thought closet.

Who led me to that truth? Was it the sweet little girl and her daddy? No, it was God's Spirit. His role is to lead us into all truth. When I was guiding my own thoughts, I was headed for a train wreck. I was quickly derailing and leading myself down a path that would further complicate my issues.

I need a better guide than my thoughts and emotions. I need God's Spirit to lead me to truth, and so do you.

Take part in your own "I Spy" game with Philippians 4:8. What is troubling in your thought closet today? What thoughts or situations are you dealing with today? Ask the Holy Spirit to remind you of truth as you fill in the following activity.

What do you spy and why? Let me start you off. I spy something true because: *I can embrace God's promise to give me strength no matter how tired I am.*

I spy something true because:

I spy something honorable because:

I spy something right because:

I spy something pure because:

I spy something lovely because:

I spy something of good repute because:

I spy something excellent because:

My friend, if we follow the leadership of God's Spirit, we trade our destructive and untruthful thoughts for those that are constructive and truthful. He is the One who leads and teaches us to know what is worthy of our thought closet and what should be sent to the Island of Misfit Thoughts.

My response to this role of God's Spirit:

Actions I will take because of what I know about this attribute of the Holy Spirit:

Before you close the book today, look at yesterday's notes you wrote and glance back at today's notes. Ask the Holy Spirit to counsel you, remind you of truth, teach you, and lead you today. Remember, no matter how crowded your thought closet may be, there's always plenty of room for God's Spirit! Great job this week!

Thoughts to ponder as you go through the day ...

Are you relying on your self-control or the Spirit's control in your life?

Which of the four roles of the Spirit do you need most in your life?

session three
LISTENING GUIDE

The woman with the issue of blood dealt with:

_____

_____

_____ _____

I am a woman with an issue of _love & my Body_

1. We must name our issue to be able to replace our _trouble spot_
   with God's _Truth_ .

2. Triggers are _events_ or _emoshions_ that cause
   your issue to grow in your thought closet.

3. Draw near to _____ .

Only Jesus can bring _____ _____ , true soul healing,
to your _____ .

Tahlis is translated *corner* in Numbers 15:38 and *wings*
   in Malachi 4:2.

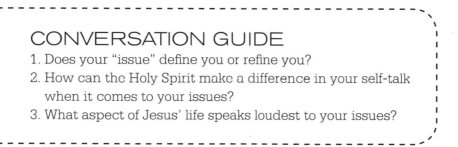

CONVERSATION GUIDE
1. Does your "issue" define you or refine you?
2. How can the Holy Spirit make a difference in your self-talk
   when it comes to your issues?
3. What aspect of Jesus' life speaks loudest to your issues?

Video sessions are available for download at *www.lifeway.com/women*

GUARDING THE DOOR OF YOUR CLOSET

"Keep watching and praying that

you may not enter into temptation;

the spirit is willing, but the flesh is weak."

MATTHEW 26:41, NASB

Sneak a peek into Patsy Clairmont's thought closet ...

Patsy Clairmont is a beloved speaker and one of the finest authors I know. When I told her about this study, she murmured an interested ... hmm. So, I asked when she discovered her self-talk was damaging.

"So many people were saying things to me that conflicted with what I was saying to myself. One of us had to be wrong! So I had to stop and say, Everyone can't be wrong. Do I trust their judgment? Am I willing to receive what they are saying is truth? If I am, then I have to change the messages in me ... the Enemy is a liar and a thief, and he comes in to set a lie in place and steal your joy."

Read more of Patsy's words at *Selftalksoultalk.com.*

Day 1
AWAKE, MY SOUL. TUNE IN!

Here's a secret from my thought closet: I have an obsession ... with the burners on my stove. I'm driven to keep them spotless. Now that I own a gas stove, this dysfunctional issue may not require therapy, but it wasn't always that way. I once hovered over the burners on my electric range—the pans, rims, and surface beneath were all targets of my compulsion.

Before you put me on your prayer list, let me explain. For the first 13 years of marriage, we lived in homes with cook-tops corroded by years of careless cooking and half-hearted cleaning. I valiantly scrubbed but to no avail. I replaced old burner pans with new ones, but I was never satisfied because under those gleaming burner pans lurked the grimy gunk from decades of apathy and neglect. Then in 1999 we moved into a 20-year-old home with a 20-year-old stove. Oh girl, thoughts about those burners filled me with dread. They probably hadn't been cleaned since 1979!

I had a responsibility to my obsession—I mean, my family—so I lifted the coils to inspect. When I felt the rims, the pans, and the surface beneath, I was stunned. There was another woman as obsessed as I was! (Bless her compulsive heart—put *her* on your prayer list.) Surgery could have been performed on that stove—spotless!

So grateful, I ended every cooking excursion by lifting the coils to clean them. I removed pans and decontaminated underneath each time, even when I only boiled water. (OK, maybe I should be on your prayer list!) I've learned something from my former obsession, though: *Keeping something clean is easier when you tend to it daily.*

The same is true of our thought closets. They need daily attention to keep them in the condition Christ intended.

What does 2 Corinthians 5:17 say about your status now that you are in Christ?

> Our thought closets need daily attention to keep them as Christ intended.

God declares all has become new! That means the old, grimy gunk is gone and you are clean, renewed, fresh … what a lovely way to think of your thought closet!

Scripture says that accessories come with your "newness." What are they?

Psalm 40:3—
Lamentations 3:22-23—
Ezekiel 11:19—
Romans 7:6—
Ephesians 4:24—

New heart, new song, new mercies—what a beautiful life wardrobe.

Do you lack or have you neglected any of the "new" belongings you wrote above? If so, circle them. On the following thought closet bins write a truthful statement you can say to your soul to reinforce what God has given you.

Now, if no one is around, just go ahead and say the things you wrote on those bins out loud! Talk to yourself! If people are around, just speak silently to yourself the phrases you wrote. That's how we keep our thought closets new and clean.

We must tell ourselves the truth about who we are and what we have in Christ. If apathy builds up, sin can crowd in. Our shine can dull and our thought closets can get awfully cluttered. We even need to talk to ourselves about our sin like the psalmist did.

What did the psalmist say to his soul in Psalm 57:8?

What is the inscription at the beginning of Psalm 57?

Friend, here's your lesson in ancient Hebrew for the day: a *miktam* was most likely a musical notation or title for psalms of penance for sin. Do you find it interesting David told his soul to "awake" in the midst of a psalm potentially about his own sin?

Why do you think he did that?

It's easy to grow dull to our own sin habits. When we aren't alert, what God made "new" can become dingy and neglected because of our sins. Sin shows up in self-loathing, negative attitudes, and accepting lies as truth, just to name a few ways. That's why we must tell our souls to be awake. When we are tuned in and alert to our sin, we can speak truth to our souls and to God about our sin.

Psalmists all throughout the collection of poetry and wisdom talked about their sin. Write a phrase to describe what they said in these psalms:

Psalm 32:5—
Psalm 38:18—
Psalm 39:1—
Psalm 51:3—

Above, check the phrases you most need to speak to your soul when you talk to yourself about your sin.

Speak that truth to your soul right now. Tuck it away into your thought closet. Now pray Psalm 139: 23-24. Ask the Holy Spirit to search you and show you if what you usually say to your soul about your sin is truth.

Write down what He shows you.

Ask the Holy Spirit to reveal if something in your thought closet doesn't belong. Do you have some sin hanging around? It could be a still-growing root of bitterness; it could be an unwillingness to embrace pure thoughts. Maybe it's self-slander. Don't write them here! Tell God, write them in a private journal, or confess them to a Bible study buddy.

Asking God to search your heart is a way to be spiritually alert. It is like telling your soul … "Awake."

The Hebrew word translated *awake* means "wake, lift up (self), stir up (self)." I like to think of it as "tuning in." With a Spirit-controlled thought closet, the Holy Spirit alerts us to the dirt in our thought closets. He convicts us of our sins.

> Asking God to search your heart is a way to be spiritually alert.

What is the action we are to take when we become aware of our sin (1 John 1:9)?

The Greek word for "confess" is *homologeo,* meaning "to assent, acknowledge." The purpose of confessing our sin to God is not to inform Him of something He doesn't know!

My friend, it's to tell God and affirm in our own hearts that we think the same way about sin as God does. It doesn't belong in the thought closet of His daughter. It just makes things dirty.

First John 1:9 tells us He forgives and cleanses. So accept His Word. The next time your feelings start to condemn you for what God has already forgiven, send those mendacious meditations to the Island of Misfit Thoughts!

When we tell our souls to "awake," we become alert to our own grime and are amazed by God's grace. To stay spiritually alert, you can't have a dimly lit thought closet. There's too much risk for dirt to gather, and it won't ever show if it's too dark in there. The light must be bright in your thought closet.

Psalm 119:105,130 tells us what light we need in our thought closets. What is it?

We must have a thought closet full of truth to fight lies, avoid sin, and stay tuned in. Keep flooding your thought closet with the light of His Word through reading it, meditating on it, and memorizing it. There is no substitute.

Day 2

TUNING INTO THE LION AT YOUR THOUGHT-CLOSET DOOR

Today is a strong coffee day! Herbal tea or decaf won't do! So grab some java, your Bible, and a pen. Here goes! Yesterday we saw we must be alert to the sin in our thought closets, but today we see we must also be alert to the Enemy at the door of our thought closets. He complicates everything. Let's assess his impact by considering these questions:

Do you tend to…
○ **naturally speak truth to your soul, or**
○ **find yourself grabbing lies and shoving them into your thought closet every now and then?**

If you still grab lies from time to time, what triggers you to do so?

Remember how I used to get so frustrated at myself, calling myself *idiot?* Even though I have tuned in and even replaced that lie with the truth, it still pops out from time to time. Why do those kinds of things still happen to us?

It happens because we have a lion at the door of our thought closets, and his impact can be devastating!

Who is the lion according to 1 Peter 5:8?

Circle the word that best describes the lion:

loud   cuddly   quiet   silent   roaring

Because our Enemy is like a roaring lion, how did Peter tell us to behave?

Why do you think Peter said be alert to a hard-to-ignore roar? Even if you're a little hard of hearing, busy, or mentally distracted, wouldn't you still notice when a lion roared? Wouldn't his threatening snarl cut through your distraction and alert you to danger? Contemplate that.

Why do you think Peter warned us to be alert to something that should be obvious?

Sometimes we can grow dull when we hear the same thing over and over. Just as a sleepy teenager can tune out the blaring alarm clock in the morning, you can condition yourself to tune out the lion's roar. But to tune out his lies is to risk continually falling for them. That's why you and I still struggle from time to time with destructive self-talk.

We have heard Satan's voice for so long that we often just assume it is our voice. Stop and ask God's Spirit to counsel you with truth about this. Do you recognize the voice of the Enemy? Are you tuned in? Do you just assume the voices you hear in your head originate with you and you exclusively?

> The Holy Spirit can counsel you about the voices you hear and help you tune in to God's.

Journal your thoughts about recognizing the Enemy's voice and what God shows you about it:

The Enemy is tricky, and we must always be alert to his voice and ways.

What did Jesus call the Enemy in John 10:10, and what are his dual intentions?

When it comes to the words you speak to yourself and the thoughts on which you meditate, how does the thief implement his plan to steal and kill?

For me, he steals my confidence and kills my peace one word and one lying thought at a time. *I'm not good enough … I can't do anything right … I'm just going to give up … Idiot!*

> Every thought we think is not necessarily our own.

Sometimes we assume that every thought we think is our own, but these destructive, lying thoughts don't necessarily come from within unless you've already given them shelf space in your thought closet. Snarly, ugly lies come from the roaring lion, our Enemy. They're his primary plan for stealing your peace and killing your joy. He knows how to drop the thought off at your thought-closet door dressed up just like something you would feel or think.

The reason I still get the urge for name-calling from time to time is because Satan knows the "idiot" word used to have prominent shelf space inside my mind. He knows it feels familiar to me, and if he growls it when I'm vulnerable, I just might grab it and shove it in my closet! Do you see his scheme?

Not every thought knocking on your thought-closet door is yours. Your Enemy is crafty and if you're not alert to his voice, you may assume those familiar words and phrases are yours. If you really start embracing truth and rejecting his lies, he'll likely get mad and desperate! Don't be surprised if he uses people to help with his sinister plan. Don't be taken aback if you hear hurtful words or insinuations hurled your way by those who have no idea the Enemy is using them to try to get lies into your thought closet. Recognize truth and recognize your real Enemy.

Write on the door at the right the words or phrases the Enemy most often tries to throw into your thought closet.

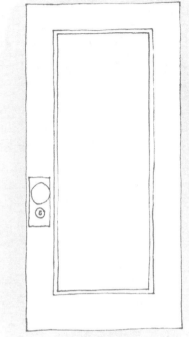

My friend, check out the useless graffiti you just wrote on your thought-closet door! Let it remind you to not just throw something in the closet because you constantly hear it. *Loser. Idiot. Airhead. Worthless.* Refuse these thoughts entry. Those ill-fitting thoughts don't come from within you. At least not until you give them shelf space. So don't let them in.

You can't always control which thoughts pop up, but you can control, through God's Spirit, what you do when one knocks. Be alert and say "no entry."

Oh girl, just because the lion keeps roaring all day—just because the destructive thoughts keep assaulting your mind—doesn't mean you have to become desensitized; and it certainly doesn't mean you have to open the door! In fact, put a big smackin' X across the door! Those phrases and words are poison, unacceptable, and unwelcome!

Let the lion roar outside the door all he wants. The more he's ignored or reprimanded with truth, the sooner he will take his dumpster designs elsewhere.

Here's the last thing I want you to prayerfully consider today: To accept lies is to reject truth. You must tell your soul to awake to sin and the Enemy. It is sin to believe lies when God equipped you to recognize and receive truth. Ponder that today. Blessings to you.

> The Holy Spirit can help us control our thoughts.

Day 3

FORTIFYING YOUR THOUGHT CLOSET

The past two days we've looked at telling our souls to awake! Today we'll consider three essential strategies to staying tuned in! These help protect and fortify our thought closet and provide what we need to prevail over the father of lies.

STRATEGY 1: PRAY

Lisa Whelchel did one of the most generous things anyone has ever done for me. She and I became friends several years ago and began to walk together with honest accountability and closeness. One day she told me how much strength she was receiving from praying warfare prayers that she read from John and Stasi Eldredge's *Captivating.* I sighed in interest and she said, "Let me read you some." Curled up on my gold couch in the living room, I remember I listened and prayed along with her, holding my cell phone to my ear. After she finished, she said, "These aren't on audio, but I want you to have them. I'm going to type these out for you so Baby Dell [my computer] can read them."

"Aren't there a lot?"

"Yeah, but I'll pray as I type."

More than 1,300 words later, Lisa had tired fingers and an energized soul! She really beat up the Enemy and kept God's attention as she stood in the gap, prayed, and typed.

Two important things happened with her gift of typing. First, she prayed. That is the primary strategy for fortifying your thought closet.

What did Jesus tell His disciples (Matt. 26:41)? Why?

The word *watch* in Greek is *gregoreuo,* meaning "to keep awake, to watch, to be vigilant"—so that you can pay attention. In other words, awake your soul and pray! Your prayer is most effective when you are spiritually alert to your own weaknesses and the Enemy's schemes.

Jesus could have said, "Pay attention and *speak truth to your soul,* lest you fall into temptation." But He didn't. Being alert to the Enemy and telling yourself the truth is imperative, but it isn't the same as "be alert and pray." Sin is tempting, and the Enemy knows it well! Do you?

Seriously, do you recognize your temptation trouble spots? ○ **yes** ○ **no** ○ **never thought about it**

Take a moment to consider your response. If you checked no or never thought about it, then think about it!

What are your temptation trouble spots?

Knowing is part of staying spiritually alert, tuning in. Never let the Enemy be more aware of your weaknesses than you are. When you become alert to your temptation trouble spots, pray, pray, pray. Prayer is our best defensive and offensive weapon. My friend, speak truth to your soul, but never let it become a substitute for prayer.

> Prayer is the best defensive and offensive weapon we as Christ followers have.

What did Jesus say He did for Peter in Luke 22:31-32 to protect Peter from the Enemy?

If Christ Himself saw prayer as a primary strategy against the schemes of the Enemy, you and I should never do less.

Ephesians 6:18 says the armor of God is completed with (check one):
○ **positive self-talk**
○ **constant prayer**
○ **staying alert with perseverance**
○ **praying only when you have issues**
○ **praying for others**
○ **isolating yourself from others**

Prayer is a simple strategy with profound results ... pray. Don't stop. My friend, pray.

STRATEGY 2: ACCOUNTABILITY

The second important thing Lisa did by typing and praying was establish agreement and accountability. We need each other. The roaring lion seeks whom he may devour, but I can guarantee you he will become a scaredy cat and think twice if he finds the *whom* he is trying to attack arms locked with a bunch of Bible-believing, praying women!

The Enemy goes for the solitary and the silent. You already speak silent words to yourself, and they can remain tools of the Enemy if you don't confess them to God and make yourself accountable to a friend. If you keep speaking silent lies to yourself, you are providing the Enemy with the weapons he most wants to use against you. Unconfessed sin and unacknowledged weaknesses are what he can use to destroy you. Don't give him weapons; give him a united front and a fight!

What does Ecclesiastes 4:12 suggest about the power of relationships?

The three-stranded cord is not "me, myself, and I!" It's you, a buddy, and Jesus. So place yourself in relationship with someone with whom you can be honest and accountable. I encouraged you to call a "Bible study buddy."

Have you done so?   ○ yes   ○ no
If so, write her name here and write a prayer of protection against the Enemy for her:

If not, ask God to reveal whom you could call and then ask Him to grant you courage. Write in the lines below your commitment to make a friend.
I will call _____ and ask her to enter into accountability with me on ___/___/___. Thank You, Lord, for giving me courage to become accountable and enter into prayerful agreement with her.

Don't isolate yourself—it isn't safe. My friend, sometimes it is pride that keeps us at arm's length from others. Can I be honest? You're not perfect and neither is the accountability buddy you desperately need. Don't deceive yourself. Allow the light of truth to flood your thought closet right now and reveal what you need most. Is it really self-protection at the expense of rich relationship? I think not. Be a big girl and call a buddy!

STRATEGY 3: FAITH

Remember what Jesus told the woman with the issue of blood? He said it was her _____ that made her whole (Mark 5:34).

Trusting God more than trusting your feelings and abilities is a preeminent strategy for protecting your thought closet against the fiery lies of the Enemy. Girl, the battle is always spiritual, and we must fight that battle with spiritual weapons.

> We must fight spiritual battles with spiritual weapons.

What does 2 Corinthians 10:4-5 tell us our weapons can accomplish?

Based on the results, do those spiritual weapons seem to be offensive or defensive?

We need to use the mighty spiritual offensive weapons to destroy lies and pull down strongholds that oppose the truth of God.

But what does Ephesians 6:16 say our best defensive weapon is?

Faith is the shield that protects us from being destroyed by the fiery darts of our Enemy. The Enemy grabs a lie from hell. It has just enough fire attached to it that it really stings. He hurls it our way with a big roar, and without the shield of faith, our thought closet is unprotected. Those fiery lies just sail right in the door and their flames remain as flickering embers, waiting for just the right (or wrong) self-talk to ignite them. The lion roars lies that often feel true. But when he roars lies, we hold up the shield of faith and speak truth!

Circle the truths that best apply to your needs today as you can stand against the Enemy's lies. These are "faith" statements, not "feeling" statements. You can hold up your shield of faith by speaking these faith statements of truth.

When the lion roars, "God doesn't listen to you,"
I say Psalm 145:18-19.

When the lion roars, "You have no value or purpose,"
I say Isaiah 43:1-2.

When the lion roars, "Your problem is unfixable,"
I say Jeremiah 32:17.

When the lion roars, "You are abandoned,"
I say Romans 8:31.

When the lion roars, "You're a loser,"
I say Romans 8:37.

When the lion roars, "You've blown it. God can't accept you,"
I say Romans 8:38-39.

When the lion roars, "Nobody cares about you,"
I say 2 Corinthians 1:3-4.

When the lion roars, "You have no willpower,"
I say 2 Timothy 1:7.

> The One who lives within you is greater than the one who roars at the door!

Girl, be alert to the real Enemy. Talk to yourself about his tactics and tell your soul to tune in. The next time he roars and throws the fiery darts of lies, hold up your shield of faith and tell the truth! Remind your soul the One who lives within you is greater than the one who roars at the door!

Now mind your strategies today. Be prayerful, be accountable, and walk by faith. Go for it!

Day 4

BE STILL, MY SOUL. CALM DOWN.

Since I've already confessed my stove-cleaning obsession to you, I guess I will go ahead and admit something else. I always thought the lovely phrase, "Be still, my soul" was actually in the Bible! I am secretly hoping you are now saying, "It's not?" Well, it's not! It's a beloved phrase that begins a beloved hymn by Katharina von Schlegel who originally wrote it in German. It was translated into English by Jane L. Borthwick and then composed by Jean Sibelius to the tune of "Finlandia." It's a beautiful hymn.

I like to sing to my soul, "Be still." It's calming at those times when the lion's fiery darts get lodged in my thought closet and I need a little relief! You may find it interesting what telling your soul to "be still" can accomplish. Pour yourself a cup of calming tea and ask God's Spirit to teach you today.

The exact phrase "Be still, my soul" isn't a scriptural quote, but the principle of being still and calming down is throughout the Bible. We must know what to say when we talk to ourselves, and telling ourselves the scriptural truth of "be still" is imperative. Evidently, that's what David did.

Turn to Psalm 131:2. What did David say he had done?

This phrase within this particular song of ascent compares David's soul stillness to what?
○ **a little child**   ○ **a submissive child**
○ **a weaned child**   ○ **a good child**

Think about why David compared his stilled soul to a weaned child. Most babies are a little cross and frustrated when the weaning process begins. It challenges their structure, their selfishness, and their security. But David compared his still soul to a child who has already been weaned.

What do you think he meant?

A weaned child is reconciled to a new way of feeding and new sources of nourishment. That's how our souls are to be. We are to reconcile ourselves to the challenge of our security, the change in structure, and the cutting off of selfishness if God so deems. Matthew Henry put it this way, "When our condition is not to our mind, we must bring our mind to our condition."[1]

The context of this psalm reveals that David never positioned himself for kingship; God anointed and appointed him. He compared himself to a weaned child because he considered himself manageable and governable by God for whatever God chose for him—whether king or shepherd.

David's comparison denotes he was well-reconciled to the position and state God saw fit. How about you? Are you "stilled and quieted" before God (NIV)? There can be no real peace in your thought closet until you are. What about some of those unchangeable labels we discussed in week 2? Have you told your soul to "be still" about that label or do you harbor a little resistance in your thought closet?

> Stilling our souls brings peace and calm into our thought closets.

The reason stilling our souls brings peace and calm into our thought closets is because it puts us in a posture of acceptance rather than anger and deference rather than defiance.

Read Psalm 46:10 and write how God expects us to behave before Him:

The original Hebrew word for "still" in Psalm 46 (KJV) pictures a physical position. It's like letting your body go limp or relaxing the grip of your hand. It simply means you quiet yourself by acknowledging He is God and His ways rule.

Do you trust Him like a weaned child trusts his mother? Do you show resolve to His ways even when they aren't your ways? Do you trust Him if He changes up your structure, your security or points out your selfishness?

Consider these questions and journal a little about them here:

Think about what you say to your soul when life changes.
Do you say, "Be still," or do you say "Be angry," "Be resistant,"
or "Be self-protective"?

> **Write down what you say most often.**
>
> "Be _____."
> "Be _____."
> "Be _____."
> "Be _____."
>
> **Circle any of the "be" phrases above that belong in
> your thought closet—that are true and constructive.
> Place an X on those that don't belong in your thought
> closet—phrases that are not true or are destructive.**

What you say to your soul matters. Those phrases get tucked
in your thought closet and you wardrobe your life with them.
Does your life show the fruit of those "be" statements on which
you placed an X? Are the tight-fitting wardrobe of control, the
drab garb of depression, the stiflingly stiff suit of legalism, or
the red-hot smock of rage sometimes the dressings of your
life because you have anger rather than acceptance in your
thought closet?

> **What are the results (fruit) of those X'd "be" phrases
> (roots) in your life? For example, if I tell myself "Be
> self-protective," I bear the fruit of being isolated or
> defensive.**
>
> If I tell my soul, "Be _____,"
> the result is: _____.
>
> If I tell my soul, "Be _____,"
> the result is: _____.
>
> If I tell my soul, "Be _____,"
> the result is: _____.

My friend, be still. Quiet your soul before God. Let the sweet
fruit of righteousness bloom from your thought closet. Accept

what He allows and trust Him with what you don't understand or prefer. Trust me, you don't want a thought closet full of anger or else you will clothe your life with its ugly attire.

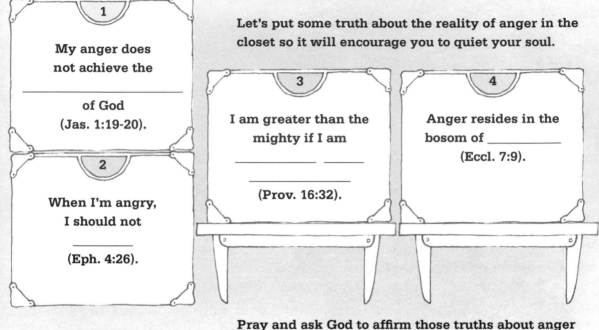

1

My anger does not achieve the

_____

of God
(Jas. 1:19-20).

2

When I'm angry, I should not

_____

(Eph. 4:26).

Let's put some truth about the reality of anger in the closet so it will encourage you to quiet your soul.

3

I am greater than the mighty if I am

_____ _____

_____

(Prov. 16:32).

4

Anger resides in the bosom of _____

(Eccl. 7:9).

Pray and ask God to affirm those truths about anger to you right now.

> Just because you don't express anger overtly doesn't mean you don't experience anger.

And may I say something to my mellow, unruffled, easy-going friends? Just because you don't express anger in an overt way, like an overheated, menopausal, stressed-out woman, it doesn't mean you don't experience anger. In fact, it would probably be wise to define what anger truly is.

How would you define anger?

The kind of anger we've been considering is the fruit of rebellion, the opposite of submitting, and the net result of selfishness. That means if we haven't tuned in to our sin and Enemy, if we have not held high the shield of faith, we most likely have the sparks of anger in our thought closets ... hmmm. Agree? Ponder that today. Tomorrow we will see what it means to have a fire in the thought closet!

Day 5
FIRE IN THE CLOSET

I've started a few fires in my illaudable culinary career. The worst was in an old oven in our home in Oklahoma. The oven didn't match our kitchen, and I really didn't like it. But it worked, so the ever-frugal Phil wouldn't replace it. And being blind, it really shouldn't have bothered me. Yet I like my appliances to match even if I can't see them! However, all that has nothing to do with what happened.

One night I used pot holders to place a dish in the preheated oven. I carefully positioned the pan on the rack and closed the door. I set the pot holder on the counter and went to another room. Within minutes, I smelled something. I hurried back to the kitchen and clearly detected the sinister scent of smoke.

I assumed some of the casserole had bubbled over. Wrong. I opened the oven door and flames leaped out. This was no sauce drip. This was an inferno! You may have noted I laid "the pot holder" rather than "the pot holders" on the counter. I was roasting the other pot holder!

Home alone, I panicked. I filled a bowl with water and sent it splashing in! As I did, I realized the oven was still on! I doused the flames, but now an ominous electrical crackling sounded and a strange new smell filled the kitchen.

I thought flour smothered electrical fires. So still panicking, I hurled the remains of a five-pound bag of flour into the embers!

Let's just say we ordered pizza that night, spent the rest of the evening cleaning the dough-like substance from every inch of my kitchen, and the blind woman and her frugal husband ended up with a brand new matching oven the very next day!

We're all like my oven. We have the potential, when under the wrong conditions, to explode.

What does James 4:1 say about our fiery potential?

> We all have desires that battle within us.

James said that we all have desires that battle within us. We all have what it takes for war to erupt and the potential for our inner volcano to blow its top. We all have the potential to ignite the smoldering embers within us and create a bigger fire. Anger doesn't occur outside our thought closet. We don't have to invite it in because the raw material is already there.

How do you think it got there?

If we don't stay vigilant in holding up the shield of faith, one of the Enemy's fiery darts can get in. Its simmering embers will stay in our thought closets, waiting to grow if we let them.

Perhaps when you tuned in to Satan's custom-made schemes, you may have determined it was anger he uses against you. When your anger rises, what you say to yourself will either be a weapon for Satan to use against you or a balm that promotes greater soul stillness.

Those internally spoken words you use at such crucial moments will be like water or like gasoline. You know what happens to a flame if its doused with water and what happens if you throw some gasoline on it.

So what do you say to yourself? What do you throw on those smoldering emotions? Do you settle yourself down with soothing words of truth or do you stoke the fire with accusations, bitterness, and self-pity?

You may want to turn back to week 1, day 5 and review the importance of words being both gracious and true as we talk about the difference between gasoline words and water words. Let's do a little closet consideration:

What kind of words ignite your anger?

What situations trigger frustration or ignite anger?

I ask you to write these down because if we are going to be spiritually alert and guard the thought closet, we must be more aware of our weaknesses than the Enemy is. Remember? Let's begin with the gasoline words you say to yourself. Make your own list of gasoline words. Here are some of mine:

> You always …
> You never …
> You should have …
> You ought to …
> And the ever popular, "Idiot!"

So write some of your gasoline words on the labels.

Gasoline words always make things worse. When we're quick to judge, to accentuate flaws and to criticize, our words make flickers burst into flames and emotions spiral.

What does Proverbs 15:1 say results from harsh words?

Can you think of a time when the gasoline (harsh) words you spoke to yourself stirred up your anger? Describe that time:

Does your soul-talk unwisely stir up inner anger? If you're not sure, then think about how you speak to others. Often those who are harsh and quick to judge others turn that same flammable intolerance on themselves. Gasoline words rarely express mercy. Don't speak those words *to* or *about* others, and my friend, please don't speak them to your own soul either. Take a moment to ask God's Spirit to counsel you in this area and guide you into truth. You may be a woman with an "issue" of anger. Jesus made the woman with the issue of blood whole because of her faith. Reach out to Jesus in faith.

Journal below what He shows you.

Your thought closet doesn't need gasoline! It needs the water of the Word. So continue in your closet consideration.

What settles you down when you feel angry (besides chocolate)?

What do you say to yourself that brings you peace?

Water words bring peace and calm. They make feelings settle down and allow emotions to find proper perspective. Water words are truthful and full of discretion, grace, and mercy. They don't condemn. They encourage and cleanse.

Truthful, refreshing water words will safeguard against fires in your thought closet and nourish the places where you feel barren needing the fruitfulness of God's truth. So take a moment and write down the water words your soul most needs to hear today. Make sure they are gracious and true.

Here are some of mine:

"You are a jar of clay with a treasure inside."
"Good try."
"Way to go."
"You are fearfully and wonderfully made."
"You don't have to be perfect."

Pen some of your water words below.

From what you know about the character of God, would He use the water words you just wrote when talking to you? If you're not sure, call your Bible study buddy and read them to her. We all need wisdom to recognize and speak truth, and we need to be accountable to our sisters in Christ to walk in truth.

> We all need wisdom to recognize and speak truth.

Are you a woman of peaceful water words? Do you rightly speak the gentle answers of truth to your soul? ○ **yes** ○ **sometimes** ○ **no**

If you checked any response other than yes, stop and ask God's Spirit to make you aware of what you say to yourself and to guide you into truth.

Don't assume hard, truthful words are not water words. We sometimes need to use scalding hot water to clean a wound, and freezing cold water prevents swelling. Water words are the same to our souls. They are always gracious and true, but they may hurt for a moment. The result is a brighter, healthier thought closet. Here's your standard: Gasoline words are harsh and do not lead to peace. Water words are truthful and ultimately make it well with your soul.

As you finish today, write one of the following passages on a note card. Meditate on it and may it keep things cool in your thought closet!

Psalm 29:11
Philippians 4:7

Good work this week.

1. Matthew Henry, *Matthew Henry's Concise Commentary on the Whole Bible* (Nashville: Thomas Nelson, 1997), 566.

session four
LISTENING GUIDE

We must be completely _____ and _____ to what is in our thought closets.

Things to know about Naaman:
He was _____.   He was _____.
He was _____.   He had _____.

Potential mess-ups in a thought-closet makeover:
_____ _____ _____

Do not allow _____ into your thought closet.

We must be willing to reach _____, and we must be willing to draw _____.

In 2 Kings 5:13 the servants were: 1. _____ 2. _____

Question 1: What do you see in my life that _____ you?

Question 2: What do you see in my life that you would like to _____ me about?

Question 3: Is there _____ you would like to tell me?

When you are ministering truth to someone you love, do it with the same kind of _____ with which you would approach Jesus.

CONVERSATION GUIDE
1. What kind of "be" statement do you say to your soul when life gets challenging? Be still?
2. What kind of gasoline words do you speak to your soul?
3. What kind of water words do you need to add to your soul talk?

Video sessions are available for download at *www.lifeway.com/women*

week
FIVE

GOD IN THE CENTER OF YOUR THOUGHT CLOSET

Bless the LORD, O my soul,

And forget none of His benefits.

PSALM 103: 2, NASB

Sneak a peek into Lisa Whelchel's thought closet ...

My friend Lisa is an actor, speaker, and author of several books including the massively popular *Creative Correction.* She's learned to remember God first in her thoughts and make Him the center of her thought closet. She's one actor who no longer rehearses her conversations or accomplishments.

"I've had imaginary dialogues in my head, between me and people whose approval I seek—the Lord has really asked me to stop having those conversations. If I want to talk about them, He asks me to turn them into prayer, a conversation with Him. I feel I can do that with Him. I can rest in the safety of how He feels about me enough to not be perfect. I think with other people and even with myself, I want to be perfect, and I will make sure I have rehearsed or thought through everything I said or want to say so that I can give that appearance. But with the Lord, I don't feel that need. I don't have to have it all together.
It really has been awareness of those inner-conversations that has helped me take my thoughts to the Lord as prayers."

For more from Lisa's thought closet, visit *Selftalksoultalk.com*

Day 1

THE LIBRARY IN YOUR MIND

English author Aldous Huxley compared our memories to private collections of literature. Your thought closet is like a library full of the stories of your life. When you pull a book from the shelf, it might produce a smile or nostalgic longings for yesterdays. Another story might invite weeping, resentment, or regret. You might even wish you could remove it.

Our memories hold countless pages of stories, thoughts, and pictures. So what does this have to do with what you say to yourself? Thank you for asking! I will gladly tell you.

Pour yourself a cup of coffee and turn to Psalm 103. What did the psalmist say to his soul in verse 2?

This week we're going to do the same; we're going to tell our souls to bless the Lord and forget not His benefits so our thought closets will be teeming with praise and profitable memories. Let's begin with "forgetting not!" Memories can be our best associates or our worst adversaries.

What do you think makes the difference between the memories becoming friends or foes?

I think our recollections become friends when we learn from them and allow them to represent God's benefits. They turn into enemies when we avoid, glorify or ignore them.

So which books should you pull from the shelves to review? Here is your guiding principle—tell your soul to look back only to what is profitable. Let's examine what that means.

On the books pictured at right, write some key words to represent some of your most vivid, shaping memories.

Some of the memories you noted are pleasant and no doubt some are painful. In my thought closet, I have one book with the word *roses* written on it. In college the professors in our psychology department invited me to their conference room and surprised me with a bouquet of roses as a thank-you for helping with a week-long seminar. One would assume I would ooze with the graciousness that Mrs. Jolly, my wonderful, proper mother, had instilled in me. But no! Instead, filled with awkward self-awareness, I wilted, mumbled a barely audible "Thank you," and quickly asked, "May I go now?" Yes, that was it—the entire conversation. Embarrassing!

At the grand age of 22, I acted like a socially awkward middle-school girl. I behaved immaturely, and I have never forgotten it! For that reason, I used to tell myself, *Idiot! How could you act that way?* That memory always had some pretty destructive self-talk attached to it, and I saw no profit or benefit.

Now that you've had a bleak peak into my thought closet, turn back to your own.

Below the books in the previous activity, write what kind of self-talk you've attached to the memory.

Is what you say to yourself, especially the painful memories, destructive or constructive?

Does your self-talk make the memory more powerful or strip it of its power?

God's benefits can be a part of both our pleasant and painful memories. If we speak truth to our souls concerning even our painful memories, we can experience God's profit.

List below the "benefits" of God that the psalmist noted to his soul in Psalm 103:

Verse 3:

Verse 4:

Verse 5:

Wow, what amazing benefits! Tell your soul to remember those benefits and look to see how they sometimes come in the packages of rough times and difficult memories.

Can you think of a painful memory that reminds you of God's benefits? Describe and note which benefit verse above best applies.

Jeremiah remembered a painful memory in Lamentations 3. He said he chose to remember (vv. 21-23). The result gave him belonging and hope (v. 24). Jeremiah showed us how to handle memories. Acknowledge the tough time. Remember God's benefit in it, and let our soul speak truth about that memory.

Do you have some dusty old books in your closet you've tried to forget because they are so painful? Pull them out and ask God to shine the light of His truth on them. He can give meaning and make even painful memories profitable.

> " 'The LORD is my portion,' says my soul, 'Therefore I have hope in Him.' "
> Lamentations 3:24

Isaiah 61:3 shows what God can do with painful memories. Write on the bins in your thought closet the meaning God can give to even your hardest memories.

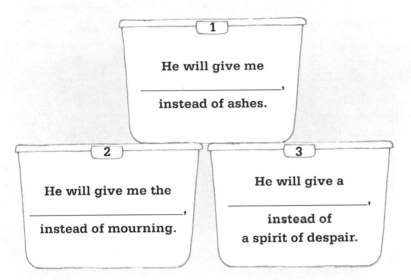

1

He will give me

_____,

instead of ashes.

2

He will give me the

_____,

instead of mourning.

3

He will give a

_____,

instead of
a spirit of despair.

Ashes, mourning, and despair—those words well describe some of our memories, don't they? But to have a thought-closet makeover, we must speak to our souls what God says about those memories—beauty, gladness, and praise!

My sweet friend, garments of beauty, gladness, and praise can hang on broken hangers. When you assign a truthful, beneficial meaning to a memory, you label it as something profitable, and it allows you to more clearly see God's benefits. If you don't label a painful memory with meaning, it will retain a negative connotation.

The meaning I finally assigned to my "roses" memory was this—yes, I felt awkward and self-aware. But I have grown to understand that as I am less self-absorbed, I am less self-conscious. God has grown bigger in my thought closet, and it helps me to keep shrinking! So, now "roses" remind me of the Rose of Sharon who blooms so lovely within me. (Isa. 35:1)

I have one important disclaimer though: When I speak of recalling painful memories, I am speaking of those you can manage. Some truly horrific memories are stowed in our thought closets and bring us utter agony—horrible situations of abuse, trauma, or cruelty. My friend, if that's true for you, please know that often those types of memories require you to seek professional Christian counseling. Do that so you can be on the path of healing.

When you look back at profitable memories, both pleasant and painful, note God's benefits. When was the last time you told your soul to "forget not"? Your soul needs such prompting. Otherwise you can too easily focus only on today, this moment, this worry, this problem. *Yet our memories of God's benefits are just as compelling and every bit as real.*

Now is a good time to give it a try. Say to your soul, *"Soul, remember the good things God has done."* Now put the rest of your world on hold for a few moments and simply ponder the thought. If you have trouble, step outside and feel the breeze, breathe in the fresh air, feel the sunlight fall gently on your skin, or listen to the chirp of a bird or the rustle of leaves in the wind. Just glance through the shelves in your thought closet. Muse over some of your memories.

> **In the space below, write some graffiti to describe God's benefits. Note memories, realities—anything that helps you remember God's benefits.**

As you go through your day, let your mind wander through the archives of memories and no matter what you recall, tell your soul: "Forget not His benefits!" May God grant great profit to even your most painful memories. Bless you.

Day 2
I WILL REMEMBER

Connor burst through the door after school and bubbled over with a tidbit of second grade inside information. "I have a secret," he gasped.

Like a dutiful sentry, he determined to guard the trust he'd been given. But I could tell he was about to explode.

"Well," he hedged, "I guess I could tell you, Mom, cause you won't remember it anyway!"

Truer words have ne'er been spoken! My fortieth birth-day arrived with a few more wrinkles and a few less brain cells! Connor's comment was fresh evidence of a memory that's lost a bit of its sharp edge. I could say the moral of the story is your secret's safe with me, but there's a deeper consideration.

We can be forgetful, can't we? Though our closets are brimming with profitable memories and God's benefits, it can be hard to recall them when our minds are crammed, lives are busy, and circumstances get difficult.

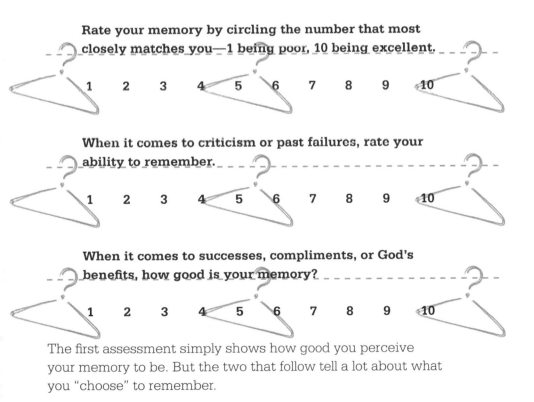

Rate your memory by circling the number that most closely matches you—1 being poor, 10 being excellent.

1   2   3   4   5   6   7   8   9   10

When it comes to criticism or past failures, rate your ability to remember.

1   2   3   4   5   6   7   8   9   10

When it comes to successes, compliments, or God's benefits, how good is your memory?

1   2   3   4   5   6   7   8   9   10

The first assessment simply shows how good you perceive your memory to be. But the two that follow tell a lot about what you "choose" to remember.

What do the circled numbers in the last two scales reveal about your true ability to remember?

What do you think causes you to remember certain things and forget others?

Sometimes we are truly forgetful and sometimes we just choose not to remember. Remembering is a discipline that takes effort and focus. That's why God commanded remembrance and even provided ways to help His people remember.

In the Old Testament Book of Deuteronomy, God urged His people at least eight times not to forget what He had done for them. He told them to remember *sixteen* times. His reminders are like sticky notes stuck on their cabinets, taped to their mirrors, and tucked in their wallets—or like sandwich boards slung over their camels!

The word *Deuteronomy* actually means second law. It was an obvious reminder—God's version of a neon sign. Let's face it, we all need sticky notes or maybe even neon signs to help us reinforce and recall God's benefits, especially when our thought closets get cluttered or dim.

What did God consistently have the nation of Israel use to prompt their memory? Read Exodus 28:9-12 and Deuteronomy 27:1-7 for a hint!

God consistently prompted His people in Scripture to remember and commemorate His benefits, most often with the use of stones. They rested on the shoulder of the ephod, acknowledging the 12 tribes. Stones were the first host of the written law of God; stones formed altars, and they were even used to represent a covenant (Gen. 31:44-54).

According to Joshua 4:3-9,20-21, what is another reason for having "stones" of remembrance?

The Israelites gathered stones from Jordan and built an altar so when their children asked, they could both remember and teach the children the benefits of God. Do you realize your memories provide the same opportunity? That's why we must tell our souls "forget not." It behooves us to glean the profit from each memory so we grant our loved ones a right assumption about the character of God, even in the painful memories.

> **Do you have an emblem or keepsake that expresses to your family the benefits of God? If so, describe it. If not, think of one. Pull it out and describe it so you can explain to your family what it represents.**

I use several things to help me forget not God's benefits and to keep my thought closet in order. One is a beautiful stone with a deep thumb-sized impression in its center. My dad used to say it was from him constantly rubbing his thumb on the rock as he worried about me. He gave it to me when I was in my teens as a reminder that I could cast all my worries on God because God cared for me.

When I began speaking and teaching, I carried the special pebble in my purse or pocket to help ease my nerves. Whenever I'd search my purse or put my hands in my pockets, I'd feel the stone, and it would remind me not to worry.

What do you use to help you remember truth and what really matters? Do you carry photos? Do you keep Scripture verses or quotes posted in your home or office?

> **Describe your memory prompts and how they remind you of God's benefits.**

> **What else could you do to prompt your memory to recall God's benefits?**

These are all simple ways to tell your soul to forget not, to look back and remember—and we all need them. Otherwise our thought closets get crammed with lies, clutter, and worries.

I don't think Asaph had pebbles in his pocket or sticky notes, but I do know he had one accessory in his thought closet that helped him to remember, and you have the same accessory—the ability to choose. He chose to remember, disciplined himself to remember, and willed his soul to remember.

> **Read what Asaph wrote in Psalm 77:6,11,12. In your Bible, circle each time he said, "I will" or "I shall."**

Five times in that short passage the psalmist exercised his volition to forget not God's benefits. Let's do the same.

> **"I will remember my song in the night."**
> **What song will you remember tonight?**

> **"I will meditate with my heart."**
> **What will you dwell on and ponder today?**

> **"I shall remember the deeds of the LORD."**
> **What deeds of God will you remember today?**

> **"Surely I will remember Your wonders of old." What wonder of God will you intentionally recall today?**

> **"I will meditate on all Your work, and muse on Your deeds." Which of God's works or deeds will you muse on today? (Psalm 77:6,11-12, NASB)**

As you answered those questions, you exercised your will to forget not God's benefits. Pause and ask God's Spirit to empower you to follow through with your choice to forget not.

My friend, tell your soul "I will, I shall" forget not God's benefits. Use memory prompts to help you speak truths to your soul and to strengthen your choice to remember. As your thought closet is filled with the truth of God's benefits, your life will be wardrobed with His character. Happy pondering today!

Day 3
GRUMBLES IN THE THOUGHT CLOSET

One of the perils of being blind is I forget people can see me. That's another good reason to tell my soul to "forget not!" This can really be a problem because I have a tendency to talk to myself out loud when I think no one is around! Thankfully, I kind of mumble, so it's not easy to understand what I'm saying.

Most of the time my mumbles go something like this: "I need to put milk on the grocery list." Or, "I thought I put my cell phone in the kitchen ... where did I put my cell phone?" But there are times when I mumble complaints.

Sometimes I stand clearly in the center of my thought closet. From that vantage point things look far less tolerable! My self-talk can be summarized: "It's all about me!" When that's my situation, I mumble things like, "I always pick up his clothes; why can't he pick up after himself?" Or, "I don't like this, I don't like that ... blah, blah, blah!"

Put simply, I grumble and mumble complaints! We all have the tendency to talk to ourselves that way from time to time, don't we? If you're not sure, listen to what goes on in the thought closets of some women: *This church never listens to my ideas. My mother-in-law is so annoying. That meal was too salty. I have nothing to wear. My house is way too small. Our car is old. He watches too much football. That preacher is boring.*

Whew! It's highly unpleasant to read those phrases, isn't it? Yet those statements symbolize what we often stow away in our thought closets. Those toxic phrases represent what we say to ourselves when we choose to grumble.

Think about what you say when you talk to yourself. Do you ever grumble? If so, about what?

Sometimes we grumble to ourselves out of habit. Maybe we have a more naturally pessimistic personality or we learned to do it. But whether it is habit, disposition ,or upbringing that contributes to grumbling, the real root is selfishness.

According to Philippians 2:3, how much are we permitted to do from selfishness?

Rather than out of selfishness, we are to act with what?
○ **good self-esteem**   ○ **self-will**
○ **low self-esteem**   ○ **humility**

Complaining always reveals a lack of humility and plenty of self-centeredness. Complaining doesn't flow from a thought closet where God is central. Our grumbles show our self-focus, certainly the ultimate cause of the Israelites complaining. But what did they name as their reasons for complaint?

In Numbers 11:1, they complained about _____.

Numbers 11:4-6, they complained they lacked _____.

Numbers 14:1-4, they complained they were _____ _____.

Numbers 20:2-3, they complained over no _____.

Numbers 21:5, they complained there was no _____, and they hated the _____ God had provided.

The Israelites grumbled about how hard their trip was, how they wished they could go back to Egypt, how there wasn't enough food, the food they got they didn't like, the water was bitter, there was no water. Ugh! Before we get too judgmental toward our ancient complainers though, review what you grumble about.

Are your grumbles more justified than theirs were?
○ **yes** ○ **no**   **Explain your answer.**

Does complaining reflect a ...
○ **sense of entitlement or a**
○ **spirit of gratefulness?**

If you grumble, what are you really telling your soul? Write your soul an honest note containing the real point of your grumbles by filling in the blanks in the letter below.

Now, girl, this is not an exercise with right and wrong answers. The answers aren't hidden somewhere on the page. Relax, use your imagination, and be honest and thoughtful.

Oh my soul, when I choose to complain, I do it because

"It's all about _____!" My plans, my needs, and my

preferences are really more important than _____.

When I throw my grumbles into the thought closet,

I plan on wearing them later as _____ or _____.

When I complain, it's really harmful, but I choose to do

it anyway because _____. So, soul, make room in

the thought closet for my grumbles by pushing out

_____.

Sincerely, _____
(your complaining companion)

I know that was a radical exercise, but sometimes we don't realize the impact of what we say to ourselves if we don't face it in all its unattractive truth. And complaining, no matter how we justify it, is just really unattractive, and it can make us very unattractive in our countenances.

In Philippians 2:14, Paul distinctly commanded us to "do all things without _____ and _____."

In verse 15 we see the results of having no complaints going in or out the door of our thought closets. What are they?

Without complaining and grumbling, you will shine brightly in the midst of our world. You will be wardrobed with the light of Christ! How lovely.

In contrast, if we are the center of a thought closet crammed with grumbling, we will clothe ourselves in the tight bright clothing of me, myself, and I! That outfit never fits well, is highly uncomfortable, and very unattractive.

Monitor what you say to yourself today. If you start to grumble, relabel that complaint with gratefulness.

Write statements of gratefulness you can say to your soul to replace grumblings.

We need to speak statements of gratefulness to our souls, not grumblings because ultimately God is the One to whom we gripe. When the Israelites grumbled against Moses and Aaron, when they complained about food and water, they were actually grumbling against God.

My sister, when we grumble, no matter what we are complaining about, we do the same. He doesn't deserve our griping; He deserves our gratefulness. As we finish today, ask God's Spirit to help you monitor your mumbles with the light of God's Word.

Write one verse here on which you will meditate to help direct what you say to yourself today. Let it, not your complaints, be the last truth you review in your thought closet tonight.

Way to go, sister … you're doing a great job!

Day 4

WHO IS IN THE CENTER OF YOUR THOUGHT CLOSET?

Over the last few weeks we've talked a lot about "what" is in our thought closets. We rummaged through and found a few labels, some ill-fitting lies, a number of faulty assumptions, lots of profitable memories, maybe a few complaints, and we've been tucking truth in there all the while! We are women on a mission to have a thought closet makeover!

Today we aren't going to focus on "what" is in the thought closet; we want to confirm "who" is in the center of it. So grab your Bible, pour yourself something warm to drink, and settle in. Ask God's Spirit to grant you discernment. We want to make God the center of our thought closets. That's what the psalmist did by speaking to his soul.

Write what he told his soul to do in Psalm 146:1.

In your own words, what does it mean to tell your soul to praise God? In your definition, try not to use common expressions such as worship, exalt, adore, and so forth. If possible, express what praise means to you without pulling out a common definition.

Do you tell yourself to do what you just wrote? If so, how often?

We need more than just a Sunday morning prompt to praise; we need a steady dialogue of praise filling our thought closets. We need to tell ourselves to lift up God; otherwise, we will naturally lift up ourselves. C.S. Lewis once wrote, "From the moment a creature becomes aware of God as God and of itself as self, the terrible alternative of choosing God or self for the centre is opened to it."

Suppose you, C.S. Lewis, and I are all sitting around sipping coffee and talking about this. Ignore the fact that I would be embarrassing you because I am an unashamedly geeky Lewis fan!

Answer the following questions from our discussion.

Lewis: So, tell me ... when did you become aware of God as God?

Your answer:

My answer? I would tell him when I was a child I came to faith in Christ and fell in love with God with all the earnest and maturity I had. But my discovery of how little I really know God as God and how deeply I want to know Him keeps growing. Sometimes I think it's a moment-by-moment recognition that He is God— a mystery, a glimpse. It's unfathomable.

Lewis: Hmmm ... you both are so profound! When and how did you discover yourself as "self"?

Your answer:

I would be trying to copy your answer without sounding too much like a desperate plagiarist! That's a hard question, isn't it? But here's what I would tell him. I most discover myself when I determine I'm not God. When I come face to face with my own frailty, with the fact that I am not in control, and I'm desperate for God's grace even to breathe. It helps me see God as God when I see myself as I truly am. When did that happen to me? Twenty years ago, and twenty seconds ago. I am prone to wander and rediscover my true self frequently.

Lewis: Wow. You women are doing well with these questions. I wish I weren't a dead author and was still writing books, I would ask you to be my co-authors. (At this point, you would pick me up off the floor and tell me to compose myself.)

So here's my last question. What have you chosen for your "center"—God or self?

Your answer:

My answer: I choose God. I want to choose God. More than anything I want God to be the center of my life—the center of my thought closet. The only way I know to do that on a daily basis is to focus on Him, talk to my soul about Him, and lift Him up rather than lift up myself. Otherwise, I naturally choose self as my center.

John the Baptist more fiercely faced the temptation to lift himself up than most any of us will.

What did he say in John 3:30-31 that gives us understanding as to how John perceived Christ?

What did John say about himself in Matthew 3:11?

In John 1:22 John was asked who he was. What was his answer in verse 23?
- a prophet   ○ the forerunner of Messiah
- a voice   ○ a big important guy

John could have answered with almost any of those names. But he called himself "a voice crying out in the wilderness." A voice. It's like saying an instrument, a guy, a tool, a woman, a mom, a wife, a daughter, a vessel. His response shows he was not the center of his thought closet—Christ was.

Who is our center is revealed by what we say, whether to ourselves or to others.

What do you say about who you are and what does it reveal about who is in the center of your thought closet?

Are you satisfied with your answer?

Let's be really practical. You can say "praise the Lord" to your soul all day long, yet somehow not place God in the center because you are already in that prime position. How do you really know if you are the center of your thought closet?

Check out these symptoms. They will help you know if you are in the lonely center.

- The cashier at the store doesn't make eye contact. Instead of feeling compassion for her, that she might be having a bad day, you think she's rude and tell yourself she doesn't like you.
- The doctor's office doesn't return your call promptly. You tell yourself it's because he doesn't value you as highly as his other *more important* patients. His tardiness has nothing to do with the fact that he may be busy or have an emergency—it's all about you.
- Someone cuts you off in traffic. Rather than recognizing we all make mistakes or sometimes act inappropriately, you react with, "What? Do you think I'm invisible?"
- No one at the party initiates conversation with you. The idea that you should make the effort to do the same just never occurs to you.
- Your spouse says, "Somebody left the milk out." You spout, "It wasn't me. You're always blaming me!" You don't notice that you were not the target of the comment.

Any of these is evidence that either you haven't discovered self as self or God as God, and you've got a thought closet full of me, myself, and lies. My friend, remember that what you really love, you focus on. What you really exalt, your thoughts always turn to.

Ask God to show you—what or who do you lift up in your life?

What or who do you exalt?

Are you in the center of your thought closet? It's lonely in there! Make room for God. Here are three things for you to do to make God the center:

1. Build a throne with praise for God to reign in your thought closet. Speak "You" statements about God rather than "me" statements about and to yourself.

2. Pray daily that you will decrease and God will increase. Ask, "Is what I'm saying right now making me or God grow bigger in my thought closet?"

3. Stay connected. Remaining self-centered is easier if you remain isolated.

> "My friend, rejoice in the LORD, O you righteous!
> For praise from the upright is beautiful" (Ps. 33:1, NKJV).

Day 5
TEMPLE TALK; WHAT TO SAY TO YOURSELF ABOUT YOUR BODY

I really don't like to exercise. Do you? You don't have to tell me. Friends don't make friends exercise or even talk about it if we don't want to! But I did have a redeeming moment on my treadmill one day. As I sweated and panted, I was listening to my Bible. In between verses, my mind would wander to other things, like my flabby arms.

I began to scold myself for not being more diligent with exercise. Then I followed my thoughts down a path of how disappointed I was that I let my weight fluctuate. I would veer off my miserable mental path every few seconds to tune back in to the Bible that was still reading in my ear. I remember distinctly tuning in just in time to hear Psalm 84:1. Now that you've got the self-talking, sweaty image of me on the treadmill in your mind, take a look at what I heard:

> "How lovely are Your dwelling places,
> O LORD of hosts!"

> "Do you not know that you are a temple of God and that the Spirit of God dwells in you?"
> 1 Corinthians 3:16, NASB

119

> "Or do you not know that your body is a temple of the Holy Spirit who is in you, whom you have from God, and that you are not your own?"
>
> 1 Corinthians 6:19, NASB

When I heard it, I began to laugh. If you don't know why I saw God's sweet sense of humor in that verse in that moment, you can look at 1 Corinthians 3:16 and 6:19.

Our bodies are the temple where God dwells. The psalmist said, "How lovely are Your dwelling places." That means that your body is the dwelling place of God and it is lovely! Is that a word you would normally use to describe your body?

Face it friends, we're women. Even the most lovely among us rarely perceive our loveliness. We obsess over our bodies, constantly concerned about our physical appearance. Whether you are a size 2 or a size 22, what you say to yourself about your temple has less to do with the condition of your body and more to do with the condition of your heart.

It is stewardship of truth to regard your temple in the same way God does. So let's have some girl-to-girl temple talk today. Keep the verses from 1 Corinthians in mind as you sit back while I tell you a little story.

Imagine your job was keeper of the temple in ancient Israel. Every morning you wake before dawn to enter the temple courts with your broom and mop. Throughout the day you are occupied with dusting, arranging, cleaning, oiling hinges, and polishing wood.

Temple maintenance is a noble commitment especially if you're doing it out of love for God. But what if you say to yourself as you sweep and polish, "I don't need to worship in this temple. I'll just spend time patching cracks in the plaster or sweeping along the baseboards. I want this temple to be the best-looking temple there is!"

So as God's people worship, you're back in the storeroom on your knees retouching the paint behind the door. Is God pleased? Might He say to you, "I am pleased you honor My temple, but the purpose of my temple is to worship Me. You have become more interested in fixing up your temple than honoring Me. "

Now leave your imaginary temple job and consider the words of Paul once again (1 Cor. 3:16; 6:19).

What did the story you just read say to you?

Are you balanced in your approach to managing and maintaining your temple? Why or why not?

Can you still bring praise to God if you neglect your temple?

Can you still bring praise to God if you obsess over your temple?

You do have a temple maintenance job! Your body is His temple and it is good stewardship to attend to your temple, to maintain it and keep it in good working order. It's even OK to enjoy fixing it up with new hairstyles and fun clothes or jewelry. But the purpose of attending to your temple is not so you will bring honor to the temple; it is to bring honor to the One who dwells in your temple.

It would be inappropriate to make your temple the object of worship, and it is equally inappropriate to discount the loveliness and acceptability of your temple—even if it is over-weight! To dishonor the temple is to dishonor God. To seek to glorify and worship the temple is also to dishonor God.

Based on the verses you've already read today, why does a deflated view of self dishonor God?

Read Romans 12:3 and Romans 11:20; 12:16. Why does an inflated view of self dishonor God?

Our body is God's temple, so we should have a right estimate of it. It is biblical for us to have a healthy view of ourselves.

What did Jesus command us to do in Matthew 22:39?

God expects us to love our neighbor in the same way we love ourselves. That implies we should and can have a godly and healthy love for the person God created us to be. Loving ourselves the way God loves us radically differs from self-centered love, though it's thinking of ourselves the way God thinks of us.

Based on the following verses, write a statement or two on the walls of the thought closet below that articulate how God values you.

Isaiah 43:1

Isaiah 43:4

Jeremiah 31:3

Romans 15:7

1 Corinthians 6:20

Ephesians 1:4

Ephesians 2:10

1 Peter: 2:9

You may need to speak those truths to your soul today. I suggest that you stand right in front of your mirror and speak each one out loud! Remember, we want thought closets full of truth, and these are truths from God's Word. They are not feelings; they are facts! As you honor His Word by trusting it more than you trust your feelings, you honor the One housed in the temple. He deserves our ultimate praise and devotion.

Stick with me while we take this "temple talk" just a step further. Paul told the Thessalonians there would come a day when the "man of lawlessness" (2 Thess. 2:3) or the "anti-Christ" would set himself up to receive the attention and worship that only Jesus deserves.

Read 2 Thessalonians 2:4. How did Paul describe the enemy of Christ?

Though it's a radical picture, it reminds me of what I do in my own temple sometimes. I set up my own throne, built brick by brick with the glue and mortar of self-centeredness. Sometimes we can get so busy and unaware that the pursuits of the temple overshadow the purpose of the temple.

Think about it. What pursuits of your temple are most important to you?

What is the purpose of your temple?

Do you ever focus too much on the pursuits of the temple and neglect its purpose? How?

Most of us get caught up in the pursuits of our temple and neglect their purposes from time to time. So let us continue to pray for God's Spirit to grant us wisdom and balance.

Write one statement you can speak to your soul about balancing your pursuit with the purpose of the temple.

Psalm 119:36-38 tells what will keep us from selfishness or vanity. Find the verses and rephrase them into a prayer to God to help you pursue balance and the purpose of the temple:

May you and I keep a healthy balance in our temples. An inflated or deflated view of ourselves dishonors God. May we maintain, steward, and care for our temples, but may we never let anyone but God sit on the throne in our temple.

My friend, you are a temple—the place where Almighty God chooses to make His dwelling. He calls His dwelling lovely. Speak truth to your soul about your temple. Does He wear you well?

1. C.S. Lewis, *The Complete C.S. Lewis Signature Classics: The Problem of Pain* (New York: HarperCollins, 2007), 566.

session five
LISTENING GUIDE

Two things you must remember to forget:

1. You are to forget your _____.   2. You are to forget _____.

Recap the bad events of the day and ask yourself:

What can I learn about _____? What can I learn about _____?

Then ask God to _____ the events of the day.

Recap the good events of the day and return them to Christ as _____.

The things in your thought closet that are tough and that you want to forget can be lumped and dropped on the _____ _____ _____.

Our thought closet cannot be full of _____ and full of _____ at the same time.

As we begin to _____ in our own thought closet, _____ _____.

You don't have to remember your sin, because God has moved it as far as the east is from the west. He's _____ and _____ it.

CONVERSATION GUIDE

1. Who or what is in the center of your thought closet?
2. When you're feeling painfully self-aware, what might you tell yourself about the focus of your attention?
3. What kinds of things do you use to help you "forget not" God's benefits?

Video sessions are available for download at *www.lifeway.com/women*

A HOPE FILLED THOUGHT CLOSET

Why are you in despair, O my soul?

And why have you become disturbed within me?

Hope in God, for I shall again praise Him

For the help of His presence.

PSALM 42: 5, NASB

Sneak a peek into Chonda Pierce's thought closet …

My friend Chonda, a much-loved comedian and author, gave me a sneak peek into her thought closet. To sort fact and feeling, she makes a list of lies and truths when she talks to herself. It's helped her speak truth and hope to her soul.

"I've had to learn to rehearse in the dark what I have learned in the light. Hopelessness needs to be on the list of lies, because our feelings lie to us, especially women. I always say that if Satan is the author of lies then depression is his cell phone because depression is based on feeling hopeless.

"But … hope is Christ. Colossians says 'I'm going to give you a secret that has been kept hidden from generations is now disclosed to the saints.' In other words, when Jesus came the secret was out. 'And the secret or mystery is this … Christ in you, the hope of glory'" (Col. 1:26-27).

For more with Chonda, visit *selftalksoultalk.com*.

Day 1

SPEAKING HOPE TO YOUR SOUL

Girl, it's week 6! Thanks for hanging in there for the whole study. How's your thought closet? Have you recognized what you say to yourself? Have you been refusing to let lies in the door? Have you relabeled those lies with truth? If so, you're well on your way to a thought closet makeover!

What's the most significant thing you "recognized" about your self-talk so far?

What lie or lies have been the toughest to "refuse?"

Which lies have you "relabeled" with truth?
Lie: _____ Truth: _____
Lie: _____ Truth: _____
Lie: _____ Truth: _____

Over the last few weeks we've talked about what I call "The 3 R's": recognize, refuse, and relabel. But actually there is a fourth R: Repeat! We have to constantly practice and repeat what we've chosen to speak to our souls. When we get tired, our emotions work against us. That's why we're going to spend our final week practicing telling our souls to put our hope in God and march on. First, let's establish what hope is.

List words or draw pictures in the margin that represent hope to you.

I remember as a child in the 70s seeing yellow ribbons tied on trees. It was a symbol of hope—someone was expecting and waiting for a loved one to return. Biblical hope involves expectation and waiting also.

Based on the following verses describe or draw what biblical hope is:

Colossians 1:27

Romans 5:5

1 Peter 1: 3

Hebrews 6:19

1 Timothy 1:1

God's Word tells us hope is an anchor; it grounds us. It will never disappoint us; it's alive, and hope is Christ Himself!

Hope is an abstract concept, difficult to explain. I may not know exactly what hope is, but I know what it does. Hope took my friend Patsy from the prison of her agoraphobia and walked with her one step at a time into arenas full of women where she speaks without fear. Even now hope takes this woman confined to the dark world of blindness and daily shines the light of quiet triumph and gentle serenity.

Hope wooed my friend Alicia, while she was an atheist, from her cold world of intellect into the warm intimacy of

> Hope is Christ himself!

knowing God. Hope sat with my friend Karen in the doctor's office when she heard "cancer" and then carried her through months of recovery. Hope took Mother Theresa to Calcutta and Martin Luther King to the steps of the White House. Hope glued Rosa Parks to her seat on the front of the bus. Hope may be what compelled you to this study. We need hope.

The psalmist told his soul in Psalm 42:5 to "hope in God." Do you do that? Do you tell your soul to place your hope in God?

Answer honestly. I tell my soul to put your hope in ...

- ○ **money**
- ○ **relationships**
- ○ **health**
- ○ **faith**
- ○ **family**
- ○ **my appearance**
- ○ **my job**
- ○ **my abilities**
- ○ **other**

> Where we place our hope is revealed in what we say to ourselves.

If you weren't sure where you tell your soul to hope, think about what you say when you talk to yourself. Where we place our hope is revealed in what we say to ourselves. "He'll never change." "I've always been this way and always will be." "I must be trim and beautiful or he won't love me."

Phrases like those seep into the thought closet and fill it with despair. Those kinds of words reflect our hope is in people, ourselves, or circumstances.

Our actions also reveal where our hope is placed. When I'm feeling particularly hopeless, it shows up in the way I eat! When I feel out of control about my weight or just stressed out, I will eat way too much ice cream and ignore my treadmill! Those actions reveal that I feel hopeless and those actions exacerbate my hopelessness.

What kind of actions reveal when you feel hopeless—actions speak at least as loudly as words.

Often the reason we lack hope is because we've unwittingly told ourselves to hope in the wrong things. When we misplace our hope, we end up disappointed.

True biblical hope, though, will not disappoint us. And that's why we need to tell our souls to hope. Scripture tells us to place our hope in three distinct places or people.

Fill in the blanks, "Soul ...

place your hope in _____ Ps. 33:18,22; 147:11

place your hope in _____ Ps. 119:81,14; 130:5

place your hope in _____ Ps 39:7; 62:5,

Go ahead, talk to yourself out loud! Placing our hope in God's Word, His love, and in Him alone makes our thought closets unshakable! My friend, when you're tired, hope in God promises your strength will be renewed (Isa. 40: 31). Placing your hope in your own efforts will only create more fatigue.

If you place your hope in God's Word, you are secure. If you place your hope in your opinion, you will be shaky and prone to being governed by emotion (Jas. 1: 7-8). Telling your soul to hope in God's love casts all fear out of your thought closet (1 John 4:18). If your thought closet was full of hope, what would the wardrobe of your life look like?

Personalize the following truths about hope. Write them on the walls of your thought closet because these are the reasons you and I speak hope to our souls.

God's _____ is on me if I hope in His love. Psalm 33:18

My hope is in God's _____. Psalm 119:81

God has been my _____ since my _____. Psalm 71:5

God takes pleasure when I _____ in His _____. Psalm 147:11

Hope brings _____ into my life. Proverbs 10:28

God is my _____, therefore I have hope. Lamentations 3:24

Hope makes me _____. 2 Corinthians 3:12

Think about where you're placing your hope. Tell your soul to hope in God, in His love, and in His Word. Hope will ground you, anchor you, and make you unshakable.

Day 2

WHEN YOUR THOUGHT CLOSET IS BLUE

In the Book of Psalms an unidentified psalmist opened his personal journal and allowed us to look on the tear-stained pages.

In Psalm 42:5, what question did he record?

Why do you think the psalmist asked this question? Check one: He was ...
○ **scolding himself for being down.**
○ **just trying to have a conversation with his soul**
○ **searching for the reason for his despair**
○ **hoping a therapist would overhear and intervene**

The first 100 or so times I read that, I thought he was reprimanding his soul. "Come on, soul ... You're not supposed to be depressed. " But his internal dialogue isn't scolding—it's searching. The psalmist surveyed the contents of his thought closet to find out why everything hanging in there was in shades of blue.

What colors make up your thought closet? Now this is a "be creative" kind of question! Think about it.

I think I have a lot of jewel tones hanging in my thought closet. I'm pretty passionate and sometimes intense. Sometimes I've got lots of fire engine red or scarlet feelings, bright sapphire sentiments and opinions, and even contemplations that take on shades of pewter or onyx! And, yes, from time to time, there's some "blue" in there and I feel down.

See what I mean? What color are your personality, your memories, secrets, feelings, treasure, and thoughts?! If you're really creative, get some colored pencils to record the shades in your closet!

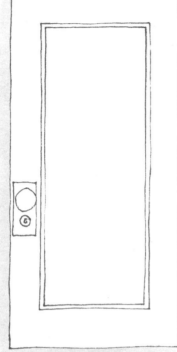

Do you have much "blue" in there? The psalmist saw a lot of blue when he surveyed his thought closet because he clearly felt downcast. Note two important things from his survey.

First, he acknowledged he felt despair. If blue feelings crowd your thought closet, they may be the same old feelings of anger, despair, or fear. You can't experience a thought closet makeover if you don't acknowledge what makes you shaky.

We need to acknowledge dark and difficult emotions. Otherwise, just as we could pull an old, unattractive dress off the hanger and wear it when we're tired or down, we'll be prone to pull them out and wear them without even realizing it.

> First, the psalmist acknowledged he felt despair.

What emotions do you need to acknowledge?
I acknowledge I feel: _____
I acknowledge I feel: _____
I acknowledge I feel: _____

Second, the psalmist's question acknowledges he was disturbed emotionally, and he asks his soul why. He recognized there was a cause for feeling downcast.

What questions do you need to ask your soul? For example: Why are you so angry, hypersensitive, or overwhelmed? Why are you down in the dumps?

Your questions:

> Second, he recognizes there is a cause for feeling downcast.

It's good to acknowledge our emotions and ask our soul questions, but don't fret. We may not have all the answers! We'll get to that. Hannah talked to herself when she was in despair.

What does 1 Samuel 1:13 reveal about the way Hannah was talking to herself in the temple?

How did Hannah explain what Eli mistook for drunkenness in verse 15?

What both Hannah and the unnamed psalmist of Psalm 42 did was very wise. They both acknowledged something was wrong. The psalmist talked to his soul and Hannah talked to God. There is a time for both. To search your soul by asking some questions gives opportunity for God's Spirit to counsel and teach you. To acknowledge you are troubled and automatically pour out your heart to God like Hannah did is also wise. Hannah didn't need to ask her soul, "Why are you downcast?" She already knew! She felt despair because she was barren.

> To acknowledge you are troubled and automatically pour out your heart to God is wise.

Given the specific condition of your thought closet, what do you most need to do today? Talk to self, talk to God, or both?

In the following letter, write to either yourself or God. First, acknowledge what may be going on in your thought closet. Next, ask your soul or God questions. And then turn back to Psalm 42 before you finish because you need to tell your soul the answer.

Dear Self or God, (circle which applies)

I acknowledge _____.
Questions I have include: _____
_____.

Psalm 42 tells me what to do. "Hope in _____."
I admit I tend to place my hope in _____.

In Psalm 42:5,11, I will claim two promises:
1. _____
2. _____

The psalmist told his soul to hope in God and I will tell my soul to do the same.

Sincerely,
(your name)

When you are confronted with a circumstance that challenges you, you have two choices. You can say to your soul, "Get depressed." Or you can say to your soul, "Hope in God." Place your expectation in the goodness of God. That's what the psalmist did. He attached his hope in God to a promise from God. He asked, "Why are you in despair, O my soul? And why have you become disturbed within me?" Then he told his soul, "Hope in God, for I shall again praise Him for the help of His presence" (Ps. 42:5, NASB). And, "I shall yet praise Him, the help of my countenance and my God" (v. 11).

Can I be totally practical with you for a moment? Verse 11 says God will be the help of our countenances. It's true. His hope can change the expression on our faces. But we can help our countenance too. Here's how.

Think about the corners of your mouth. Now lift each corner toward your cheeks. Wider, bigger, brighter! There you go! You just helped your countenance by smiling! It's easier to be downcast if your face is frowning, grimacing, or grumpy. Trust God more than your feelings and smile because your hope is in Him, not your situation.

What have you said to your soul lately? What you say is stored in your thought closet and broadcast on your face. When you are confronted with a disappointment or a bad situation like that of the psalmist and Hannah, do you throw hopelessness into your thought closet? Do you assume the worst, focus on the down side, or worry yourself with, "What if?" When you are dealing with hopelessness or are overwhelmed, what do you typically say to your soul?

> **Write where the psalmist asked God to lead him when he was overwhelmed (Ps. 61:2).**
>
> **To what rock do you need to go when you feel overwhelmed? (See Matt. 16: 15-18 for the answer.)**
>
> **Read Matthew 16:16. What did Peter confess about Christ?**

The truth that Jesus is the Christ, the Son of the living God, is our rock also. When we feel overwhelmed, hopeless, or emotionally shaky, we too go to that rock. Jesus is our Rock.

He grounds us and is the anchor for our souls.

My friend, hope is what we tell our souls to "do" even if we don't "feel" it. Practice telling your soul that today and smile as you see that the feelings of hope will follow your choice to hope!

Day 3
A SONG IN YOUR THOUGHT CLOSET

Pour yourself some coffee or tea, and let's transition today. We talked about the importance of telling ourselves to hope in God. Today we'll explore telling our souls to march on like Deborah did. Turn to Judges 4 to read Deborah's story.

> **The prophet Deborah led Israel when they were enslaved by a ruthless Canaanite king named _____ (4:2). His military commander _____ (4:2) rode roughshod over the Hebrews for _____ years (4:3). Hearing from God that the time was right to throw off the chains of slavery, Deborah commanded her general, _____, (4:6) to muster his army. The plan was for him to lead a force of _____ men (4:6) while Deborah's smaller force marched in plain site of Sisera's army, luring them smack into Barak's men! Deborah was ready to press on because she had heard from God Himself. Barak, however, wasn't so sure (4:8). And can we blame him?**

Facing a daunting task—particularly one that involves risk, sacrifice, and pain—can make the best of us want to wave a white flag. Maybe Barak thought his militia would be defeated and humiliated for yet another generation. That would be a pretty good reason for him to quit even before he began. We've all faced enemies and battles that reveal our frailty and make us feel feeble, overwhelmed, and ready to turn tail.

Describe such a "battle" or experience in your life that made or makes you want to give up:

When you are in the midst of a thought-closet makeover, sometimes you feel like you're fighting the same old battles all the time. Just when you get a victory, the battle rages again! Even as I've been writing this study, I still catch myself saying things to myself that aren't true. How frustrating!

Sometimes you feel like just throwing in the towel. *Is it really such a big deal? Saying these things to myself is just me, my inner dialogue. There are much bigger sins to deal with!*

But what you say to yourself really matters because you really matter. Renewing your mind with truth is worth the battle. God loves us, and His standard, what is acceptable to Him, should dictate what we say to our souls. We just can't quit because we get tired or feel a tinge of hopelessness every now and then. You may not "feel" equipped for the battle, but you are equipped.

> God's standard, what is acceptable to Him, should dictate what we say to our souls.

One of the reasons for Barak's concern could have been what is noted in Judges 5:8. What is it?

Do you feel like you can identify with underarmed Barak? That kind of lack of weapons can make anyone afraid to battle.

In the battle over your thoughts and self-talk, what kind of weapons do you have (2 Cor. 10:4)?

Ephesians 6:13-17 describes your wardrobe for battle. What does verse 17 say is your best offensive weapon?

Your weapons are spiritual. The most reliable weapon you possess is the sword of the Spirit, which is God's very Word! Because your weapons are fully trustworthy, you can trust them to help you whatever battle you face. So don't give up.

In spite of his shakiness, Barak stepped up to the challenge. But he refused to go without Deborah. She agreed, but under one condition: When the Israelite army won, Barak would not be given credit for the victory.

Instead, Judges 4:9 says the victory would be credited to a _____ (hum the Rocky theme song here).

Let the battle begin! Deborah sent Barak to initiate the battle, and "at Barak's advance, the Lord routed Sisera … and Sisera abandoned his chariot and fled on foot" (Judg. 4:15, NIV). In other words, Sisera ran for his life. Utter celebration swept through the people of Israel. The victory had been won! They were free! And in response to this stunning victory, Deborah and Barak broke into song.

The new hit song swept across the liberated land. The lyrics are recorded in Judges 5. In verse 21, what does Deborah confidently sing to her soul?

> Singing to ourselves keeps our thoughts focused and our spirits motivated.

In the midst of Deborah's song, she spoke perseverance to her soul. "March on, my soul; be strong." Well, actually she sang to her soul. I love that thought because I too sometimes sing to myself. Do you?

One of the songs I sing to myself is "Jesus, You're my firm foundation, I know I can stand secure … I put my hope in Your Holy Word." It keeps my thoughts focused and my spirit motivated.

What are some songs you do or can sing to your soul to help you persevere and keep hope alive?

People in Scripture sang. There is something peculiarly sweet in the songs of the sons of Korah. Turn to Numbers 16 to see from whence the sons of Korah came.

What do verses 8-11 tell you about their patriarch Korah?

What was his role?

What was his grievance?

Korah's role was to serve the tabernacle and lead God's people as he ministered. But Korah wanted more. He strove for the priesthood.

How were Korah and his comrades described in Numbers 16:24-25?

○ **Misguided souls**   ○ **Nice guys**
○ **Weak willed cowards**   ○ **Wicked men**

Shamefully, Korah and his fellow rebels were called "wicked." It's hard to imagine anything good growing from a family tree with such dangerous roots.

What happened in Numbers 16:32-33?

The earth opened and swallowed Korah, his people, and his goods. What a tragedy! What a family tree!

Now turn to Numbers 26:10-11. What fate did the sons of Korah meet?

Saved from the lowest depths of the pit, the sons of Korah did not die. Eventually, they "were over the work of the service, keepers of the thresholds of the tent ... had been over the camp of the LORD" (1 Chron. 9:19). What a stewardship!

My friend, no matter what memories are stored in your thought closet, even if you feel like there's lots of failure, regardless of your present circumstances, no matter what your past ... you must sing. If the sons of Korah still had songs after such a jaded past, you must too.

You must persevere. You have no idea how God will choose to use you. Look how he used the sons of Korah.

Think about that and answer the following questions:

What would the world be lacking if I quit?

What would I show my family by giving up?

What am I settling for if I choose to give in when it gets tough?

Of all the psalms the sons of Korah sang, few are more precious to me than Psalm 84.

Rephrase the following verses of the Psalm into lyrics you can sing to your soul.

Verse 1

Verse 2

Verse 4

Verse 5

Verse 7

Verse 10

Verse 11

Verse 12

My friend, those lyrics must fill your thought closet, so sing them to your soul! They will help you persevere ... before the battle, within the battle, and after the battle.

Day 4

STEPS TO TAKE AS YOU MARCH ON

One night I found Clayton lying on his floor in despondency when he was supposed to be finishing an English project. I asked in disbelief. "Are you already done with your portfolio?"

He groaned. "I haven't started! Mom, this is too much. I'm too tired. I just can't do it."

He was paralyzed by a project that seemed bigger than he was, and instead of forging forward, he was ready to quit. I got down on the floor with him, feeling utterly helpless to motivate him. No pep talk from Mom would change one thing for that boy that night. And that's the hard truth.

When there's no hope in your thought closet and your motivation is running on fumes, you need more than just a song to sing to your soul, you need a first step out of your dilemma. "March on, my soul" isn't just an abstract concept. To march anywhere you need to put one foot in front of the other. You need a concrete plan. While you're singing to your soul, keep these three steps in mind as you march on.

1. TURN YOUR FEELINGS INTO ACTION

If you feel overwhelmed because a project is due, do the project. I know that sounds too simple. But sometimes real answers are simple. If a circumstance intimidates you, take a deep breath and confront it. Instead of ruminating about your feelings, do something—even if it seems like a small something. Take a step.

> **Read Exodus 14:16,21-22. What happened before the water of the Red Sea parted?**

When God led the Israelites through the Red Sea, Moses lifted his staff and the water parted. However, when Joshua led the Israelites across the Jordan River, there was a different strategy.

> **Read Joshua 3:8,14-17. What happened just before the water parted?**

On Jordan's bank, God instructed the priests to take a step into the water and then the water parted.

> **If you were one of those priests, how do you think you would have felt about stepping into the rushing water?**

If governed by feelings, they may have never taken a step.

> **When you are governed by feelings, how hard is it for you to take steps of perseverance? Explain.**

My friend, we must be governed by the truth of God's Word. When we speak His Word to our souls, we are willing to turn our feelings into action and walk by faith.

> **Is there an area of your life where you know you need to "take a step?" If so, write your commitment.**
>
> I will: _____
>
> **Pray: Lord, please help me to trust You more than my feelings.**

Feelings are real, but they aren't all based on reality, and they certainly aren't all productive! So, don't let them lead you. Someone wisely observed, "Nobody trips over mountains. It is the small pebble that causes you to stumble."

Oh sister, most things, most feelings, most people, most circumstances are pebbles. March on. If you pass all the pebbles in your path, you will step right over the mountain.

2. AFFIRM YOUR TRUE IDENTITY

Recognize that who you are and what you struggle with are not the same thing. Just because you have failed at something doesn't mean you are a failure. Keep telling yourself the truth about who you are. And remember, you find out who you are not in magazines, not on TV, not from the opinions of others, or even in your own self-assessment.

How do you determine your true identity?

You affirm who you are in God's Word and His Word only. When you talk to yourself about your true identity, it will always begin with *I am*. Remember, *I am* is not the same as *I do* or *I feel*. I hope your thought closet is full of truthful *I am's* based on who He is. (See p. 36 for reminders of who you are.)

> **What you do and how you feel may loom large in your thought closet. But what really counts is who you are. Affirm your true identity and then act on it.**

> **What "I am" statement do you most need to say to your soul today? I am** _____.

Keep saying that to your soul today. It will help you march on!

3. TELL YOUR SOUL TO REST.

Rest can protect us from quitting just as much as perseverance can. The Book of Exodus reveals when the Israelites were cornered by the pursuing Egyptians, they were seized with panic. Instinct probably sent them into the "fight or flight" mode—and they were ready to scatter like a flock of pigeons.

> **What sends you into an emotional "fight or flight" mode?**

> **Turn to Exodus 14:13-14. What did Moses command?**
> ○ **attack the enemy** ○ **stand still**
> ○ **run and hide** ○ **call your mother**

Though I'm all for calling mom, Moses told the people, "Do not be afraid. Stand still, and see the salvation of the Lord" (NKJV). There are times when victory comes from "standing still." Think about the emotional "fight or flight" situation you described.

> **Is God telling you to stand still?**

> **If so, what could be accomplished by your stillness before Him?**

Now read Exodus 14:15-16 (HCSB). What did the Lord say to Moses? "Tell the Israelites to

_____   _____ .

Sometimes we need to stand still while we wait on God. And sometimes we need to move on, to get up, and to start marching. Both are acts of perseverance.

Do you need to march on through your "fight or fright" situation?

If you did persevere, what could be the result?

We all need the balance between telling our souls to rest in God and march on. In Psalm 116:7, the psalmist told his soul to rest. God provided for our strength and protected our stamina in His commands to His people to rest.

What do the following verses tell you about the importance of rest?

Exodus 23:10-11

Exodus 34:21

Leviticus 23:3

My friend, God clearly commands rest for people, even for the land. If the dirt needs a rest so it can be productive and keep on persevering, fulfilling its calling, so do you.

Consider the following questions:
1. Do you need to speak rest to your soul?
2. What brings your soul rest?
3. In what areas of your life do you need to rest instead of rev?

Be a woman of wise steps. Your Heavenly Father will help you turn feelings into action. Remember, your Bible study buddies can help you discern productive feelings also. When you receive wisdom to help you monitor your thought closet, you will have so many *I am's* on the shelves that you can't help but be wardrobed with your true God-given identity.

Really knowing who you are will help you keep hope in the thought closet and perseverance as your song. When you speak truth to your soul, you will experience the godly balance of knowing when to rest and when to rev ... the result will be knowing when to hum Brahms "Lullaby" and when to whistle the William Tell Overture. "Hi ho, Sister!"

A wise penguin in the movie *Happy Feet* declared, "Triumph is just trying with a little 'umph'!"[1] I love that. Wise penguin. If we combine our effort with power, God's power, we will sing a victory song just like Deborah did!

But let's be practical. What do we do when we feel overwhelmed and ready to quit?

Day 5
WHEN TO TELL YOUR SOUL TO PRESS ON

Oh, my friend! This is our last day together. I long for you to have a thought closet full of truth, where God is the center. So I'm pulling out my best dark chocolate and drinking my favorite coffee as I write this last, special day.

We often think we most need to speak perseverance to our souls when we are on the brink of defeat or at the end of our ropes! Of course, speaking truth to our souls then is essential, but it is no less essential in a surge of sudden prosperity. Being at the end of this study, enjoying the liberty of a tidy thought closet, is a great time to tell your soul to march on. Why? Because if we keep telling ourselves to persevere and have hope when we're winning, we'll sing the same song to our souls when victories are hard to find.

The moments following great victories may be the most vulnerable moments you face. After persevering and speaking strength and hope to our souls, we tend to set that all aside to bask in the warm glow of sweet success. We feel tired, and we relax. We let down our guard. We dim the light in our thought closets and slip life into cruise control. And we are in peril beyond our understanding.

What did Solomon warn in Proverbs 6:10 and 24:33?

We must guard ourselves against the wrong kind of rest! If we invite mental laziness, spiritual sluggishness, a relaxed attitude or complacency into our thought closets, we can be under surprise attack before we know it.

Part of the way we experience "folding of the hands" and being less vigilant is by reducing our commitment to community. You have enjoyed a group for several weeks now and just because the study ends does not mean your relationships should. Staying connected keeps you marching on and protects you from the enemy's attack.

What happened to the Israelites on their way out of Egypt (Deut. 25:17-18)?

The Amalakites attacked the liberated Israelites. But they went for a certain part of the group.

According to these verses, why were the feeble ones lagging behind?

The Israelites had been on quite the exodus from Egypt. Talk about emotionally and physically exhausted! The Enemy attacked the ones who were lagging behind, straggling, cut off from the majority of the group. They were weary and worn out. This Enemy didn't go for the strong ones or the ones up front, marching forth in victory and confidence. No, this Enemy, like the Enemy of our souls, went for the weary, the stragglers, those who were tired and barely hanging on. The stragglers were no doubt disconnected from the group.

You see how important it is for you to remain connected even when this group study ends. What kind of commitment can you make to stay connected?

Write it here with the date.

In the margin write a prayer of commitment and plea for God's help to fulfill your commitment to stay connected.

When we are physically and emotionally spent and worn, we become susceptible to the Enemy's attack. We become an easy target. As a result of a fatigued soul and body, our Enemy attacks us with despair, depression, impatience, lies, and self-condemnation. So it's critical that we speak rest to our souls and stay connected. But we are also in peril of burning out and melting down after a victory.

The lesson of Deborah's song is to sing songs of strength to your soul when the battle wages and even when you've won. When you've received the answered prayer, the promotion, the opportunity, the success, keep right on singing ... March on, my soul, be strong! Don't stop now. Don't falter.

The habit of perseverance will protect us after the battle, after the triumph, when we could easily have an "Elijah episode." Turn to 1 Kings 18:19. We pick up the story as Elijah speaks to King Ahab. Meanwhile, the prophets of Baal and Asherah along with the wayward Israelites are gathering on Mount Carmel.

Which statement best captures verses 23-39?
○ **Ahab whined, false prophets dined, Elijah was kind.**
○ **Israelites sang, false prophets sprang, Ahab was hanged.**
○ **Israel wailed, false prophets failed, and Elijah prevailed.**

Elijah was victorious. Now read 1 Kings 19:2-3.
What was happening to Elijah in these verses?

Elijah was on the run from one woman. He stood against 450 false prophets, saw fire from heaven fall, but even so, he was terrified and ran.

What did he pray beneath a juniper tree (v. 4)?

Elijah had just had an earthshaking, mountaintop experience on the peak of Mount Carmel. Yet he prayed, "I have had enough, Lord … Take my life." He had been firing on all cylinders, and now he had a meltdown. Elijah went from the height of the mountain to the depths of the valley.

Exhausted, which is often how we feel after a mountaintop experience, Elijah curled up in a fetal position under a tree in the desert and slept until an angel woke him and made him eat (2 Kings 19:5-8). He was strengthened by that food, and he was able to do God's work. My friend, never ignore the importance of tending to the basic needs of your "temple": eating, moving, and resting. The great prophet was tired, hungry, and emotionally drained. All motivation killers. All triggers that make us feel as if we too have had enough.

What does this say to you?

Give yourself time to rest and revive your energy before you assume the worst and give up.

Have you ever had an "Elijah episode"? I had one several years in a row. I used to call it "Dark November." I was so tired, burned out from traveling and writing, and it usually came to a terrible low around the end of November. It took wisdom, discipline, and accountability to prevent it from happening again.

What about you? Describe your Elijah episode.

Can you determine what triggered it for you?

How can you prevent it from happening in the future?

The great Physician isn't only a healer, He's also into preventative medicine! That's why He established the Sabbath and a myriad of other commands to protect us and to promote abundant life.

Based on what you've studied over the last six weeks, write out a prescription for keeping your thought closet healthy and balanced.

Elijah was a shaky, post-victory mess. He was singing the blues. He was tuning up for his own swan song. Surely, as a good Hebrew man, he knew the words of David: "He put a new song in my mouth" (Ps. 40:3). That's what the man of God needed—
a fresh, uplifting melody streaming from his thought closet like the song Deborah sang ... we need the same.

My friend, the situations can vary in your life, and they will, but the song must stay the same. You must speak and sing perseverance to your soul.

Your thought closet may still have a few old labels and some faulty assumptions that keep trying to take root. You certainly have had and certainly will have times when you just want to give up—quit the discipline of speaking truth to your soul. But don't quit. Remind your soul to focus on the finish, not your flaws and failures.

You've done a great job with this study and you've finished well. Now keep it up ... Way to go!

Finally, be strong in the Lord and in His mighty power (Eph. 6:10).

1. "Happy Feet" by Warner Bros. Entertainment Inc. © 2006.

session six

LISTENING GUIDE

When you interview yourself, you're going to look at four areas.

1. The _____ Leg

2. The _____ Leg

3. The _____ Leg

4. The _____ Leg

The spiritual leg is the only _____ weight-bearing leg of your table.

We want thought closets that are:

_____

Full of _____ _____

Full of _____

CONVERSATION GUIDE

1. If you get shaky when your "table" isn't balanced, which leg usually needs attention?
2. What practical things help you persevere in your faith?
3. How does being in community with other women help you?

Video sessions are available for download at *www.lifeway.com/women*

HOSTESS TIPS

Based on the gift they have received, everyone should use it to serve others, as good managers of the varied grace of God. If anyone speaks, |his speech should be| like the oracles of God; if anyone serves, |his service should be| from the strength God provides, so that in everything God may be glorified through Jesus Christ.

1 PETER 4:10-11, HCSB

STEPS FOR LEADING THIS STUDY

Step 1. Begin publicity four weeks before the first session. Inform participants if childcare is provided and if participants will pay for their books.

Step 2. Order member books and the leader kit that provides the videos.

Step 3. Reserve a meeting room, a TV, video player, and a CD/tape player.

Step 4. Complete your lessons in the member book and view the video session ahead of the group.

Step 5. Enlist a hospitality assistant to greet the women, prepare name tags, and plan refreshments. Also enlist a prayer assistant. Give the names of group members to this person and ask her to pray for each person before the first session.

YOUR ROLE

1. Thank you for taking on the role of hostess. I have called you a hostess rather than leader because the goal is to make women feel welcome, important, and ready to receive truth from God's Word. Think of your role in that way.

Think of the group process as you would invite someone into your home. You would welcome them at the door, take their coat and after small talk, usher them into your living room or kitchen where conversation gets more personal.

2. By hosting, you are providing essential leadership to the group without having to be the content expert. You make the group process welcoming and safe for each member.

Your role is not to teach but to provide and model warmth, facilitate the opening time, pray or ask someone to pray, show the video, and help keep the group conversation within your time-frame. You will also want to encourage each participant to enter into account-ability with other Christian women.

3. As you begin the study, you will need to explain the general flow of the group experience. Members need to know what to expect and what is expected of them in the group.

- Your role as a hostess will not only be to listen to what is shared but also to help the group manage their time together.
- Always affirm women's comments even when you don't agree. Use "Thanks for sharing, anyone else ..." when one is dominating. Expect God's Spirit to lead the group into truth. The questions in the Hostess Guide do not always demand an objective answer.
- If a group member begins to talk about wacky theology, graciously thank her for sharing and ask for input from others so the Holy Spirit can use the body of Christ to minister truth.
- If a group member chooses to remain silent, allow her to do so with comfort.

4. Each week remind members to bring their show-and-tell item from their closet for the following week's session. Jennifer gives instruction for these items in the final video segment each week. We call that segment the outro.

INTRODUCTORY SESSION

Before the Session

Ask the Holy Spirit to make His presence known during each session and as each member studies during the week. Praise God for inhabiting His Word and being the living Word. Confess any sins that hamper growth in your faith. Pray for each group member by name and by need.

Make yourself familiar with the bonus material on disc 2. It includes a music video, an interview with Travis Cottrell, and sneak peaks into the thought closets of Kathy Troccoli and Lisa Whelchel.

During the Session

1. Welcome group members individually. Introduce yourself.

2. Ask women to introduce and to share something about themselves.

3. Introduce Jennifer by briefly sharing her story (see p. 4). Explain that members will get to know her better through the next six weeks of study.

4. Distribute member books to each participant. Read Jennifer's Introduction on page 5.

5. You may choose to review the Table of Contents. Explain that the text is interspersed with learning activities to help the reader pause and apply the concepts just taught in the text.

6. Ask for questions or comments about the study. Remind group members that you, the hospitality assistant, and the prayer assistant will be praying for them during the week. Also encourage them to call you if they have questions.

7. Show the introductory video segment.

8. Lead the group to discuss the conversation guide questions from the viewer guides. You may not be able to cover all the conversation guide questions each week. Remember that they are to help your group discuss what they are learning. Do not feel that you must complete them all.

9. Encourage group members to complete their daily lessons beginning on page 8.

10. Close with prayer, thanking God for the members of the group.

11. Remind members to bring in or wear the oldest pair of shoes from their closet!

Your group members can get a free copy of Jennifer's song "Let the Words" on CD or by download.

Visit *www.JenniferRothschild.com/words* for a printable page of coupons you can distribute in your next meeting.

SESSION 1: WHAT'S IN YOUR THOUGHT CLOSET?

Before the Session

1. Find a recording of the hymn "It Is Well with My Soul" or the lyrics of the song.

2. Pray for each group member by name.

During the Session

1. Welcome group members. Distribute nametags if necessary.

2. Play "It Is Well with My Soul" as you begin to focus attention on the session. If you cannot find a recording, read the words slowly and ask members to think about the words to the hymn. Ask members to respond to the phrase, "It doesn't have to be well with your circumstances to be well with your soul."

3. Lead the group to pray for the Holy Spirit to teach them during the session.

4. Have a fun time of show-and-tell with members showing the shoes they brought. Say: "Let's watch the video and see Jennifer's shoes." Watch the video of session 1 together. Ask members to complete the listening guide on page 31.

5. Use the conversation guide questions from the listener guide to help the group discuss and apply the content from the video teaching.

6. Don't forget to come back to the video for Jennifer's parting thoughts.

Extra Material

If your schedule permits or if you are using the book without the video, use the following tools to guide discussion of the homework for the week.

- What "I am" thought has been in your Thought Closet the longest? Is it true?
- Turn to page 16 and share answers to God's Thought Closet. Ask: "In what ways does your thought closet need to look more like God's?" With each member using her own name, read aloud Psalm 139:1-4 (see p. 17).
- We learned more about self-talk, or meditation, in day 3. What are some of the things you meditate on (p. 20)? Colossians 3:2 tells us where to fix our minds. Ask someone to read this verse.

Choose an "I am" statement from Scripture to speak truth to the women in your group. If you can, find individual verses for each member. If not, find one verse to share with the entire group. Say: "God spoke 'I am' statements about Himself in Scripture. I chose _____ to share with you." Read the verse. Close by saying: "That is what is written on you as living stones!"

Remind members to bring something from their closets that they know should really be stored somewhere else.

SESSION 2: FILLING YOUR THOUGHT CLOSET WITH TRUTH

Before the Session

Secure a poster board and markers if a board is not available in your meeting room. Write on it the three principles of roots and fruits, found on pages 49-51. Leave room below each principle for answers shared in the session.

During the Session

1. Welcome group members individually. Tell them how glad you are they are at the session. Pray together.

2. Show the item from your closet that does not belong, and ask members to share their items. Say: "Let's watch the video and see what Jennifer brought in from her closet." Watch the video of session 2 together. Ask members to complete the listening guide on page 54.

3. Use the conversation guide questions from the listening guide to help the group discuss and apply the content from the week's study and the video teaching.

4. Don't forget to come back to the video for Jennifer's parting thoughts.

Extra Material

If your schedule permits or if you are using the book without the video, use the following tools to guide discussion of the homework for the week.

- Say: "Let's focus on truthful labels that come directly from God."

- Have members take turns and read through the list on page 36 to help us remember that God is the source of truth in our lives.
- Have someone explain the difference between fact, fate, and faith labels. Ask: "How do they affect us? Which do you prefer to have? Which do you usually assign yourself?"
- Ask: "Why do we cling to our faulty assumptions rather than cling to the truth? Which faulty assumptions do you need to drop today?"
- Display the poster board with the three principles of roots and fruits. Ask members to share what they discovered during their study and write answers on the poster board.
- Say: "We will now speak a truthful statement about who God is. We wrote these on page 53."

Close the session with prayer, encouragement to complete their lessons, and a reminder to bring in something that identifies them next week.

SESSION 3: A WISE THOUGHT CLOSET

Before the Session

Secure a poster board and markers. Write on it the four snapshots Jennifer helps us to explore in days 4 and 5, pages 68-73.

During the Session

1. Welcome group members individually. Pray together.

2. Share with the group the item from your closet that identifies you. Encourage members to do the same. Say: "Let's watch the video and see what is in Jennifer's closet that identifies her." Watch the video of session 3 together. Ask members to complete the listening guide on page 76.

3. Use the conversation guide questions from the listening guide to help the group discuss and apply the content from the week's study and the video teaching.

4. Don't forget to come back to the video for Jennifer's parting thoughts.

Extra Material

Use the following optional tools to guide discussion of the homework for the week. Let the Holy Spirit direct you to spend as much time as necessary on needs specific to your group.

- Ask: "How can we receive God's wisdom?"
- Review the study of Esau, David, and Sarah (p. 58). Ask how they showed their lack of wisdom and what the

potential outcome could have been if they had used God's wisdom (pp. 59-60). Ask if any group members can relate to these characters and what we can learn from their stories.

- Ask: "What does it mean to fear God? What did you learn about fearing God from the study in day 2?"
- Say: "This week we studied about the woman in the New Testament who had "an issue of blood. She also had other issues that clouded her view of herself as well as others around her. What are some issues we carry with us? How do you let issues define you?"
- Ask: "How can the Holy Spirit make a difference in your self-talk when it comes to your issues? What aspect of Jesus' life speaks loudest to your issues?"
- Display the poster board with the four snapshots from pages 68-73 as a visual means of guiding the discussion about God's Spirit. Ask for volunteers to share what they learned about God's Spirit in this study, especially about the role of the Holy Spirit and how they will act on the truth they learned.

Close the session with prayer, encouragement to complete their lessons, and a reminder to bring something dirty, stained, or in really bad shape next week.

SESSION 4: GUARDING THE DOOR OF YOUR THOUGHT CLOSET

Before the Session
Write on a poster board the three strategies we studied in day 3, pages 86-89.

During the Session
1. Welcome group members and lead a time of prayer.

2. Show the group the dirty or old item from your closet that you brought in. Invite members to show their items as well. Say: "Let's watch the video and see what Jennifer needs to purge from her thought closet." Watch the video of session 4 together. Ask members to complete the listening guide on page 100.

3. Use the conversation guide questions from the listening guide to help the group discuss and apply the content from the week's study and the video teaching.

4. Don't forget to come back to the video for Jennifer's parting thoughts.

Extra Material
Use the optional material to guide discussion of the homework for the week.

• Say: "Sin isn't an easy subject to talk about, but it is important to address." Ask members to look up the verses in Psalms, on page 81, and read when they've found the verses. Share any thoughts or feelings about what these verses say.
• Ask: "How is Satan like an enemy, a lion, or a thief?"

• Display the poster board. Say: Jennifer teaches us three strategies to protect and fortify your thought closet. They are listed here on the board. How can these strategies be effective fortification?
• Ask: "What kind of 'be' statements do you say to your soul? What kind of 'be' statement do you need to say to your soul?"
• Ask: "How do you respond when God asks you to 'be still'? Do you put up a fight? What other words would you rather use than 'still'? How do you 'be still'?"

Let the women know how proud you are of their hard work. Encourage them to continue with their daily lessons. Remind group members that next week they are to bring in something from their closets that is precious to them.

SESSION 5: WHAT YOU TELL YOUR SOUL TO FORGET

Before the Session
Remember to pray for each member during the week. Be sensitive to the Lord's leadership to send notes of encouragement or show other acts of thoughtfulness to group members.

During the Session
1. Welcome group members and lead a time of prayer.

2. Show the item you brought from your closet that is precious to you. Invite members to share their items. Say: "Let's see what Jennifer brought this week." Watch the video of session 5 together. Ask members to complete the listening guide on page 124.

3. Use the conversation guide questions from the listening guide to help the group discuss and apply the content from the week's study and the video teaching.

4. Don't forget to come back to the video for Jennifer's parting thoughts.

Extra Material
Use the optional material to guide discussion of the homework for the week.

- Say: "Our week's study began with the topic of memories. What makes the difference between memories becoming friends or foe? Which memories do we tend to have? Why?"

- Ask someone to read Isaiah 61:3. Say: "This verse redirects us to focus on God and not the painful memories. How?"

- Say: "God urged His people not to forget His benefits. What did He have the nation of Israel do to prompt their memory? What do you do to help you remember how God has worked in your life?"
- Ask: "How does a woman keep a healthy balance between loving herself and loving God?"
- Say: "In day 4 we changed our focus to 'what' is in our thought closets. In your own words, what does it mean to tell your soul to praise God? Did you have difficulty in creating a definition without using common expressions?"
- Have members share their answers to the proposed conversion with author C.S. Lewis (p. 116). Read the questions and ask members to respond.

Close the session with prayer, encouragement to complete their lessons, and a reminder to bring something from their closets that represents hope.

SESSION 6: INTERVIEWING YOUR SOUL

Before the Session
Give some thought to what your group might do to celebrate having completed the study together. Consider watching the conversation between Kathy Troccoli, Lisa Whelchel, and Jennifer in the bonus material on disc 2. Might you have a celebration dinner together? Be creative and plan to help your group end with joy and a commitment to continue their spiritual growth.

During the Session
1. Welcome group members and lead a time of prayer.

2. Share with the group the item you brought that represents hope. Let volunteers share the items they brought from their closets. Say: "Let's see what Jennifer has in her closet that represents hope." Watch the final video session together. Ask members to complete the listening guide on page 148.

3. Use the conversation guide questions from the listening guide to help the group discuss and apply the content from the week's study and the video teaching.

4. Don't forget to come back to the video for Jennifer's parting thoughts.

Extra Material
Use the optional material to guide discussion of the homework for the week.

- Ask group members to volunteer to read Colossians 1:27; Romans 5:5; 1 Peter 1:3; Hebrews 6:19; and 1 Timothy 1:1. Say: "These verses define biblical hope. True biblical hope will not disappoint us."

- Referring to day 3, ask one person to read 2 Corinthians 10:4 and Ephesians 6:13-17. Then ask: What kinds of weapons do we have to do battle over our thoughts and self-talk? What is our best offensive weapon?
- Ask someone to share their rephrasing of Psalm 84 (found in day 3, p. 138).
- Discuss the three steps from day 4. As you discuss step 1 (Turn your feelings into action), read Exodus 14:16,21-22. As you discuss step 2 (Affirm your true identity), ask: "How do you determine your true identity?" If you have time, refer to the "I am" statements on page 36. As you discuss step 3 (Tell your soul to rest), read Exodus 14:13-14. Ask, What does it take to "stand still"?
- Have members share their prescription for a healthy and balanced thought closet, found on page 147. Ask group members to share how they will keep themselves healthy and balanced after the group sessions are finished.

Pray for one another to keep a healthy and balanced thought closet.

Other Studies by Jennifer

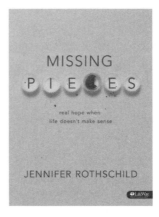

HOSEA: Unfailing Love Changes Everything

7 sessions

The Book of Hosea—it's a deeply personal and passionate love story, yet it's a difficult story. As an account full of harsh judgment unfolds, we find in its midst a rare and pure gem: the truest and purest of loves, the unfailing love of God for His wayward people, and for all people. Hosea, an Old Testament prophet, preached his own life message using his marriage as the sermon illustration. The message of Hosea is this: if you're lost, God will find you. If you're ashamed, He'll cover you. If you've wandered off, He'll come get you. Understand and apply the message of the prophet of unfailing love.

Bible Study Book   005727067
$12.99

Leader Kit   005727068
$149.99
   Contains DVDs & Bible Study Book with leader helps

MISSING PIECES: Real Hope When Life Doesn't Make Sense

7 sessions

Does God care? Is He fair? Is He even there? Although you may know all the right answers, they don't always feel right. Explore these and other questions in this realistic look at the messy, mysterious uncertainties of faith. God's ways don't always make sense, but He is trustworthy. Come close to Him. Experience unexpected peace despite your heartache. Trust Him more than your feelings. God will reveal Himself to you and fill in your missing pieces.

Bible Study Book   005371621
$12.99

Leader Kit   005371622
$149.99
   Contains DVDs & Bible Study Book with leader helps